D1155199

Be Your Own Therapist

-

Whoever You Hire Is Just Your Assistant

by Thayer White

Purple Paradox Press

Box 347172, San Francisco, CA., 94134

Grateful acknowledgement is made for permission, given by Angeles Arrien Ph.D., for inclusion of the Maori drawing from Dr. Arrien's *Cross Cultural Values and Transpersonal Experiences* module at External Program, Institute of Transpersonal Psychology, Palo Alto, California.

Some of the artwork in this book is from Lotus Smartpics for Windows. © 1991 Lotus Development Corporation. Lotus and Smartpics are registered trademarks of Lotus Development Corporation.

Publisher's Cataloging in Publication
(Prepared by Quality Books Inc.)

White, Thayer
      Be your own therapist : whoever you hire is just your assistant
/ Thayer White
      p. cm
      Includes bibliographical references and index.
      Preassigned LCCN: 94-69007
      ISBN 0-9643375-8-4

      1. Self-help techniques. 2. Psychology-- Popular Works. I.
Title.

BF632.W45 1994   158.1
                             QBI94-2190

158.1
W588

10 9 8 7 6 5 4 3 2 1

Acknowledgments

To those friends, colleagues and family members who have made such a real difference in the contents and production of this book, my heartfelt thanks to each of you: Angie, Barry, Bob, David, Eileen, Helen, Katherine, Kathi, Kirsten, Liz, Lou, Luann, Maria, Mark, MaryEllen, Pauline, Roz, and Sheddon.

To other past and present teachers here on Earth School, especially parents, peers, and clients: I continue to be surprised at how effective you were and are at providing me with so many growth opportunities. My feelings of gratitude toward you are sincere but also have been mixed at times with wistful thoughts such as, "Did you really have to be so generous with the growth opportunities?"

I do thank you all. You have given me more than you know.

Table of Contents

*A journey of a thousand
miles of change
begins with a choice to take
a single step.*

*Author's modification of famous
words by Lao-Tzu 6th Century B.C.*

Introduction

DOING 90+% OF THERAPY YOURSELF

My 23 years of experience with a variety of therapists and therapies, both as a therapist and as a client, convinced me long ago that more than 90% of the work in effective therapy could be done outside the therapy hour.* But it was not at all clear what that 90+% might be or could be. All too often I, and almost everyone else I knew, drifted in a limbo of uncertainty, ignorance and denial about personal growth paths apart from our favorite therapies.

I intend to give you, the reader, the means to set and accomplish growth and healing goals specific to you, whether or not you are currently paying a therapist.* If your paid therapist has objections to a joint discussion of growth and healing goals, perhaps it is time to examine and discuss your relationship with that therapist.

> **CAUTION:** This book is **NOT** for you if you now are (1)carrying any severe psychological diagnosis such as schizophrenia, multiple personality, etc. or are (2)in a severe crisis or in some danger of harming yourself or others.
>
> If (2) exists, take action now. Suggested alternatives are, in recommended order: (a)talk to a local helper (such as a therapist) preferably one who is already known to you, (b)call a local (or national) hotline or (c)call your local law enforcement authorities.

POPULAR IDEAS MAY BE HARMFUL TO YOUR HAPPINESS

In this book I intend to challenge many popular unhappiness-causing ideas and to support "wrong" views of such ideas, perhaps occasionally causing offense. I consider this necessary. For the areas of our lives that contain unhappiness will usually only be changed by challenge. Many popular ideas of today are unhappy ideas. If you hold such unhappy ideas, the ultimate goal of inner peace is not attainable. I hope that you, the reader of this book, will be able to discard some of your unhappy ideas while reading it.

How you respond to seemingly "wrong" ideas is important, for many of us tend to throw out the baby with the bathwater. If thoughts like "he should know better" or "that is stupid" float through your mind, you are making judgments. A more neutral response like "I don't agree with that" is a happier non-judgmental choice.

Have you ever noticed that your negative judgments about people or ideas either (1)make you unhappy or (2)serve as largely unsuccessful attempts to boost your low self-esteem? Therefore, do you really want to judge others? (See Chapter 8 for more on judgments and the unhappiness that results from making them.)

The result of our people-judgments is that we often throw away someone's ideas because they are voiced by the wrong person or because we don't totally agree with all their ideas. Just because I may espouse a few seemingly wrong ideas does not mean that everything I say is useless. I doubt that there is a person alive who will agree with everything I write in this book. When you find yourself not in agreement, I recommend that you (1)enjoy the differences between us, (2)play with my ideas mentally, and (3)evaluate which of my ideas you might like to have (even if they seem impossible/wrong today).

EMPOWERING YOURSELF

One of my goals is to empower you, the reader, to accomplish more personal growth and healing. Part of that empowerment is to realize that the therapist does not really run the show. If a client really wishes to heal, grow and change, the therapist can help.   Otherwise, the therapist is at a great disadvantage.

All too often clients presume that the therapist knows what is best for them and knows the answers; more often than not, that is just therapist and client wish-fulfillment.* If you are thinking about hiring someone or have already done so, I suggest you read Chapter 18 titled *Therapists and Therapies.*

Upon hearing the title of this book, one therapist friend remarked that I would not be popular with some of my colleagues. We laughed together, for both of us knew that popularity had never been my strength nor was it my goal for this work. Instead, for both myself and the reader, my goal is movement along our individual and collective paths toward inner peace.

May this book help you along
your road to inner peace.

*See Appendix A

This licensed counseling professional that you hired is your assistant.

To see your own therapist, look in a mirror.

Chapter 1

Using This Book

HELP FOR <u>YOUR</u> PROBLEMS?

This book can most likely help with any of your problems that therapy might help. That would include difficulties with relationships, phobias, anxieties, addictions, self-esteem, depression, co-dependency, sexuality, anger, violence, or any other problems or symptoms that are amenable to psychotherapy. There will be suggested paths to try or suggested ways to gain a different perspective, either of which will often be enough to significantly shift a given problem.

Please understand the need for some patience. Our problems and symptoms are there for very sufficient reasons, and few will be instantly cured by any means.

> <u>Reminder.</u> **This book is NOT for you if you are in crisis, in danger of hurting yourself or others, or carry a severe psychological diagnosis (see page 1 of previous chapter).**

WE ARE LIKE FIXER-UPPER HOUSES

Most of us consider ourselves to be "just fine except for that one problem" that is difficult to deny (or 2-3 problems). "If only that one would clear up, things would be almost perfect!" Actually, the vast majority of us experience dozens and dozens of unhappy/ upsetting/ irritating events every week. *Each of these is a potential handyman project for us.* Psychologically we are like fixer-upper houses, structurally sound but showing needs for a variety of repairs.

When you read this book, you may discover seventy-five or more potential growth areas for yourself. Do not feel badly about such a large number, for most everyone else is in the same condition. Most of these "repairs" can be at least partially completed by you without help from a paid therapist. Each one that you are able to accomplish will leave you feeling calmer and more able to enjoy life. But each takes time. Therefore, give yourself permission to take as much time as *you* need, years if necessary.

LET ME BE YOUR GURU
(Please remember to send lots of money.)

Sheldon Kopp's book title, *If You Meet the Buddha on the Road, Kill Him,* most succinctly expresses my beliefs about the value of most gurus. Thinking of ourselves as The Knowledgeable Ones is a thought trap into which therapists sometimes fall. Understandably so, for there is knowledge (about ways of being happier and feeling better) which hopefully we possess in greater quantity than those whom we serve. On the other hand, I do believe there are a few genuine useful gurus out there. I think true gurus have many attributes in common with Gandhi: they are not in the business of acquiring money or materials, and they preach neither fear nor judgments. If these attributes fit your guru, then perhaps you have found the real thing.

The more I do the work of therapy, the less I seem to know what path is right for clients (i.e., how to be their guru).* Yet, I seem to be effective in assisting them to find their own individual paths. While as a country we tend to be supportive of some individualism, this acceptance is limited. Unique individuals in pursuit of very different lifestyles often find their unhappy ways to my office. Frequently they are unhappy because they are trying to fit some societal, family or personal norm that is totally inappropriate for them as individuals. For example, loners often get little acceptance from society or even from many other therapists. Yet, for many loners, being alone is not only their preferred mode but their best mode. The question for them is not, "When are you going to become more involved with people?" but instead, "What is the right level of aloneness for you?".

If you have read this far, you have already exposed yourself to some different ideas and beliefs that may require sorting, sifting and detailed examination. A frequent reaction of my clients to therapy sessions is thinking about the session for many hours afterwards. This book can affect you, the reader, similarly. If it does, then you are already on the road to becoming your own guru, doing 90+% of your personal growth work (i.e., therapy).

FOLLOW YOUR OWN YELLOW BRICK ROAD

There is no right or wrong way to use this book. In fact, there are many choices available to you. There is no need to go page-by-page from beginning to end, though that is a likely choice for many. If that approach appeals to you, fine! But allow yourself to change your method if that feels more appropriate later. If one of your important growth goals is to be more creative and spontaneous, then do not follow the straight path from the first page to the last. Instead, find your own path, one that is just as suitable and distinctly more fun.

I suggest that you allow yourself to drop this book for periods of time and pick it up later when that impulse strikes. Many of my early readers chose to read it that way, reading one to three chapters with time between reading sessions. Many changes described herein can take some time to accomplish. Therefore, reading about more and more possible changes for yourself may not be productive if you are already mind-juggling prior possibilities. We only can change a few things about ourselves at a time.

If strong negative feelings develop toward me, the author, then perhaps you are attempting to "shoot the messenger" in hopes of denying the accuracy of the message. I hope that you use the book your way, and at your own pace. If you can discard some ideas (there will likely be parts of this book that you sense are presently wrong for you) without losing others that could be valuable, then you will gain the maximum. I hope to help your growth process with this book, but you ultimately are your own therapist.

FIND YOUR OPTIMUM THERAPEUTIC FOCUS

Do you enjoy quizzes about yourself and discovering the "right" answers to such quizzes? Such quizzes are often found in your favorite

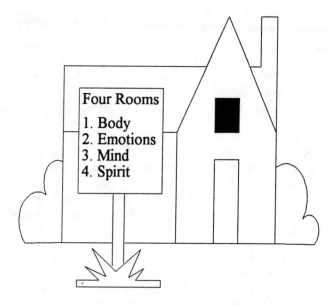

Four Rooms

1. Body
2. Emotions
3. Mind
4. Spirit

The Four-Room
House of Human Existence

magazines. If you enjoy them, take the quiz in Appendix A-- NOW! You will find the "answers" throughout the book marked with *. Of course, there really are no right or wrong answers to most of the questions. But certain answers cause us comfort and ease while others cause us grief and unhappiness. We do have choices about whether we think A or B. A significant portion of some thinking therapies (see Chapter 8) is helping clients to change their thinking from A to B, from unhappiness-causing reasoning to happiness-causing reasoning. Such therapies work!

Human existence can be considered a house of four rooms, the rooms of (1)the body, (2)the mind, (3)the emotions and (4)spirituality. Therapies usually concentrate on just one or two of these rooms. Yet for maximum health, it has been stated that we need to visit each of these rooms every day*, if only briefly.

If you have selected a therapy that concentrates exclusively in one or two rooms, you do need to be aware that your growth may be happening in only one or two rooms. You need to make a decision about how much, when or if the other rooms are visited. Ultimately, any one-room focus will likely need to change (tomorrow, next month, next year or several years in the future). There are times when focusing upon one room is entirely appropriate, and I do not intend to imply that you should select only a four-room therapist. Chapters 3-11 discuss these four rooms in more depth. **If you would like to test yourself vis-a-vis these four rooms, then go now to Appendix B.** A New Zealand Maori drawing test (which most people find fun to take and surprisingly accurate) awaits you there. It will usually show your current inclinations toward each of these four rooms. The results of this test may suggest to you that you might alter your focus to other areas.

BEING YOUR OWN THERAPIST

My goal is not to get you to change but to empower you to change, if that suits your purposes. Frequently there are choices A and B, in which choice A, though very popular and often judged as correct, leads to unhappiness.* Choice B, however unpopular, is a growth choice that ultimately leads to calmness and lack of stress. With my clients and with you, the reader, my goal is to show you such choices. I fully accept your choice and clients' choices to retain unhappiness. However, I do hammer clients over the head with such

All great truths begin
as blasphemies.

George Bernard Shaw 1919

(Author's note- small
truths too.)

unhappy choices. For they (and <u>you</u>) are the ones choosing to retain the unhappiness by continually selecting unhappy choice A.

For example, men in this culture historically have made the choice not to feel sadness and grief (i.e., choice A). The result is a wide array of acting-out behavior such as unreasonable anger or drug/ alcohol/ sexual/ gambling addictions. Such behavior temporarily relieves the stress that arises in situations that potentially might trigger sadness or grief. If such men learned instead to accept their feelings of sadness and grief, then the <u>experience</u> of such feelings (i.e., choice B) would change those so-called "bad" feelings to ones of contentment and OKness. (Please read Chapter 9 for more about this choice.) *To be your own therapist, you must first have knowledge of the existence of such choices so that you can make them consciously.* There may be many possible choices for you to make as you read this book; each will have repercussions in terms of your health and happiness.

Knowledge of what various therapies are trying to accomplish is often lacking in clients. How in such cases could clients have personal power? Therefore, just knowing what therapy is trying to accomplish can often be a significant step toward its accomplishment. Consequently, two major focuses in this book are on (1)what therapy is trying to do and (2)how you, the reader, can do as much of it as possible.

I do not intend to imply that all your growth work can be done without the aid of a therapist. Instead, do as much as you can and use a therapist as an adjunct/ assistant for what you can't accomplish by yourself. Sometimes assistants know more about certain issues than the boss. The wise boss accepts that without believing either that the assistant is boss or that the assistant knows everything. Remember that you, not the therapist, are the ultimate boss.*

THERE ARE MANY CHOICES

Even if you choose not to pursue the quiz path described earlier, it is my intention that while reading this book you will be exposed to many beliefs and ideas that in this culture directly cause discomfort and angst. The choice will be yours whether you change any unhappy beliefs that you possess. But first you must see that there is a choice.

When the world was considered flat, there was no choice. It was "obviously" the truth. Just look at the flat horizon! When the idea was then raised about the world being round, there was instant rejection by all those who "knew better". Over time, however, the arguments for roundness were more persuasive and beliefs changed. This is the same process that may happen when you meet one of my "wrong" (or blasphemous) pronouncements. Your worst response may be instant rejection, for then you may never see if it might have an inkling of truth or be preferable for you. Your best response would be to acknowledge there are at least two choices, your way and my way. That is the first step of changing, to realize (without beating ourselves up in any way) that there is another alternative to our unhappy upset responses.*

BEING GRATEFUL AND APPRECIATIVE

One recurring attribute of people who have happiness (or inner peace and contentment) is the attribute of being grateful and appreciative for what is all around them. This is an attribute that all of us could well cultivate, for it changes how we feel. Our upsets tend to melt in the face of gratefulness. This is completely contrary to the current media emphasis on what is wrong. That emphasis is unhappy, so why would I want to limit myself to just the problems? Why not emphasize some good stuff too? Therefore, throughout this book, I have included sections that can elicit these positive feelings within us. Just feeling some of that gratitude and appreciation will be a touch of healing (i.e., self-therapy) for us all. Try reading aloud the following (note how soothing such self-talk feels):

CELEBRATION TIME

The large amounts of new information about therapy give me many possible personal growth choices never before available. I appreciate that. We each have the capacity to get rid of more mental garbage than ever before. I feel grateful about that. I also feel appreciative of _____.

RECOMMENDED TESTS FOR YOU NOW (if not already completed):

Self-Help Quiz in Appendix A

Maori Drawing in Appendix B

With or without use of a paid
assistant, I hope that
when you finish
this book that you will be
able to say with satisfaction:

*See Appendix A

Creative
Natural Healing
Activities

 *Nature*

 *Writing*

 Music

 Drama

 Dance

 Art

Chapter 2

Gain, No Pain

SPONTANEITY, CREATIVITY, PLAYFULNESS, FUN & LAUGHTER

Can you get more of these sparkling qualities into your life without painful therapy? Typically, yes! There are ways to maximize them, often without having to delve into old traumas that lurk within.* This chapter provides *generally* painless ways to promote the treasures of spontaneity, creativity, playfulness, fun and laughter.

As it is now, when therapy is over, people have frequently just become less unhappy. Often missing is the sparkle that emanates from people who are in the business of fully living their lives. Part of the reason for this is that therapists rarely, if ever, receive any training in how to elicit sparkle. One assumption by some therapies and therapists is that once clients face trauma in treatment those shining attributes will somehow automatically emerge. The obvious lack of those attributes in many who are post-therapy points out that assumption's fallacy. In fact, a frequent conflict of my clients (most of whom have been in therapy before) has been the desire for more of these qualities versus the reluctance to permit their full emergence. Such reluctance stems from both fear and ignorance.

CHANGING FEAR AND IGNORANCE

To change fears may take therapy, either with or without a paid therapist. Four typical fears are: (1)I can't trust my spontaneity because I might do myself harm, (2)I won't be accepted if I laugh hard or play joyfully, (3)Creativity is often the work of the devil and (4)I fear I won't be accepted if I

*Men's happiness in life
is the result
of man's own efforts.*

CH'EN TU- HSIU 1918

enjoy myself because there are starving people in Africa. Most of us learned such fears as children. Therefore, these fears may take some therapeutic work. Chapters 8-11 will provide some means of eliminating such fears. Seeing them as unwanted and invalid, however, can be an important therapeutic step toward their elimination. (I have not included "love" on the previous list of sparkling qualities, because fear and trauma are usually present in those lacking love. For more on manifesting love, see Chapter 9.)

This chapter will try to change ignorance, which may be all that is required to allow the flowering of more spontaneity, creativity and fun.* Three common ignorant unhappy beliefs are: (1)If I face my traumas, pleasure will automatically follow, (2)I can't be happy until all my traumas have been resolved and (3)It is wrong to experience fun or to be playful since there is so much pain and suffering in the world. If you have any of these unhappy beliefs, changing them is essential. Perhaps all that will be required is to consciously recognize them as wrong for you.

> **Growth Exercise.** Try right now to jot down why you may have lost the attributes of spontaneity, humor, laughter, creativity and play. Parents, churches, schools, work environments and societal pressures are typical "causes" of such losses. You may discover a few beliefs that (1)were incorporated in childhood without conscious thought and (2)conflict with the expression of these positive qualities today. Ask yourself if you still believe that way today. If there is significant trauma instead of just ignorance associated with creativity, spontaneity, fun and laughter, these qualities will be more difficult for you to manifest.

Frequently, the first growth step is to acknowledge the conflict within, between the old unhappy (often unconscious) childhood belief and the conscious adult belief of today.

> **Growth Tip.** Create your own list of positive sayings and repeat them aloud often. "I deserve play," "Creativity is one of life's exquisite spices" and "Laughter is OK" are examples of happier adult beliefs that counter old childhood training. Even the old "every day I am getting better and better" can be valuable if oft repeated. Whenever the old unhappy way arises, it is useful and frequently therapeutic to reaffirm consciously such happier adult beliefs.

IMAGERY

The book, *Creative Imagery* by William Fezler Ph.D., is highly recommended. Just by following along with his images, your creativity and *joie de vivre* will flourish. As a sample, read the following *Creative Imagery* Beach Scene (Fezler 1989, 45) <u>into your tape machine</u> and listen to it several times, creating in your mind your own images:

> "...You are now going to take a sensory voyage. You are going to construct a scene in your mind's eye so vivid it will be as if you are actually there.

> You are walking along the beach. It's mid-July; very, very hot; five o'clock in the afternoon. The sun is getting low on the horizon although it has not yet begun to set. The sky is a brilliant blue, the sun a blazing yellow. Feel the heat from the sun against your face; feel the warmth of its rays against your skin.

> You are barefoot. Feel the hot, dry sand beneath your feet. Walk closer to the water. Feel the wet, cold, firmly packed sand beneath your feet.

> Hear the beating of the waves, the rhythmic crashing, back and forth, to and fro, of the water against the sand. Hear the loud, high cries of the gulls circling overhead."

The above is just one small sample, which I hope whets your appetite for more. Practicing images can prove invaluable in the promotion of creativity, spontaneity, fun, playfulness and laughter. I recommend Dr. Fezler's book for two additional reasons: (1)it teaches self-hypnosis and (2)it explains other ways for you to help heal yourself of all sorts of psychological difficulties.

APPRECIATION TIME

(It is recommended that you read this paragraph aloud, with feeling.): I am grateful that as a culture we have come so far from Puritan seriousness. I appreciate and value creativity and spontaneity, my own and others. I appreciate_____(express your own).

I-WANT-LISTS

Throughout this book, references at the end of chapters will be made to your I-Want-List. Because humans are naturally goal striving mechanisms, it is preferable for us to have goals. Be cautious, however, about what goals you set. They may come true in unintended ways. Please read Appendix E for ideas associated with setting goals. Without goals, or with inappropriate goals, we often founder or flounder.* I have seen a number of clients for whom goals initially are non-existent or impossible. They suffer as a result because of lack of direction. Such clients usually had unhappy experiences with inappropriate goals.

It is important for you, the reader, to also read Appendix C. For there are several ins and outs about this I-Want-List method of change that can make or break its effectiveness in helping you to manifest change. Your old unwanted pattern will likely persist if you have too many I-Wants on your list or if you do not (1)write the I-Want down, (2)say it aloud, (3)post it where you can see it and (4)reward yourself publicly (see Appendix E). Which of the following do you want to add to your list?

I want more creativity, spontaneity, fun and play in my life.

I want to enjoy humor, my own and others.

I want more pleasure in my life.

---

*See Appendix A

*The <u>useful</u> molehills of
psychological knowledge are
often obscured by the mountains
of psychological claptrap
now available.*

Chapter 3
Psychology (K.I.S.S.)

K.I.S.S.= KEEP IT SIMPLE STUPID
(directions from me to me)

I shall try to keep it simple, and hopefully interesting, this very brief but quite necessary discussion of psychology.

Post Traumatic Stress = instant simplified diagnosis of the 97% of us who grew up in dysfunctional families (see Chapter 16 for more about our dysfunctional families). Almost all of us suffer still from unhealed traumas suffered at the hands of both parents and society during our first 18 years.* We currently reveal unresolved stress from these traumas by the symptoms that erupt when our trauma buttons get triggered.

If you broke a bone in your arm, you would expect treatment from the doctor similar to treatment you would receive for a broken leg, wrist or foot. You would understand the treatment because you understand the root problem, a broken bone. For the wide variety of psychological symptoms, however, a general understanding by clients is commonly lacking about underlying roots. The roots of most symptoms have much in common with each other, though the symptoms themselves may be very different. The concept of root traumas, obvious and not-so-obvious, can provide you with a general understanding of what therapies are often trying to explore.

THE NATURE OF TRAUMA

By definition, emotional trauma is "emotional shock producing a lasting effect on a person" (*Oxford*, 1980, s.v. "trauma"). This implies that whoever is traumatized is and has been stuck in shock since the traumatic event. No shock = no trauma. Evidence for this shock is the presence of

*Animals can also
be traumatized.*

unexplainable symptoms that often result. Such symptoms include unexplained rages, fear of abandonment, blaming/ judging of others, sudden tears, sickness, phobias, anxieties, sexual dysfunctions, sleep difficulties, bouts of depression, recurrent negative behavior patterns and loss of memory.*

<u>**Not-So-Shaggy Dog Story.**</u> Let me use Pol, my then 10-month-old golden retriever, as an example of trauma shock. Pol was a frolicsome high-energy dog without fears, not even of cars or big rigs. Despite my efforts, one day he ran from a warehouse straight into the path of an oncoming station wagon, breaking his leg. He suffered obvious physical pain from the time of the accident until about 24 hours after his first surgery. During that surgery a temporary pin was inserted in his leg. For the next month after the surgery he was still the same frolicsome high-spirited dog, and <u>he showed no fear of cars, trucks or station wagons!</u> Where was his memory? Then he went into surgery again for removal of the pin, during which sodium pentothal ("truth serum") was used as an anesthetic. Afterwards, as he was being led down the hall toward me, he was obviously still under some influence of the anesthesia as he wobbled along drunkenly. When he saw me, his legs gave way and he collapsed on the floor. His whole body shook fearfully, strongly and almost violently, as I stroked him gently. His eyelids fluttered and his eyeballs moved in the same manner as when he dreamed. After approximately one minute of this shaking, stroking and eye movements, his fear and shaking subsided. He opened his eyes and picked himself up to leave the clinic. Immediately upon opening the outside door, a truck went by noisily, <u>and he was afraid!</u> Great!

But what had happened? Pol's experience directly parallels those of people in automobile crashes. They often lose memory of the crash, also memory of events near in time to the traumatic event. They too will sometimes regain memory when they become ready to face the feelings that were too painful and abundant at the time of the crash. This also happens to those who are doing significant early childhood work in therapy. Their memories of many early events are regained (or expanded in many details) as they face the traumas involved.

What is locked up in the shock of trauma? Words, emotions, sensations and thoughts are four important prisoners incarcerated by partial or complete loss of memory.* Freeing any one of these prisoners will help to heal the trauma. **The concept of a trauma knot may be useful, a knot in which words, emotions, sensations and thoughts are all intertwining strands within the knot.** Depending upon the size and complexity of the knot, loosening one or two strands may or may not completely untie the knot (permanent healing).

YOUR WISH IS MY COMMAND

A more subtle traumatic process is far more common than the abusive or shocking processes we think of when the word trauma is mentioned. Yet this more subtle process is just as damaging and often much more difficult to overcome. It is trauma. It is more difficult to overcome, because we often deny its existence or because to recognize it would cause us significant additional emotional distress.

An example of less obvious trauma is next. A parent who considers anger at parents to be unacceptable will not permit such anger by the child. The child recognizes this lack of acceptance of anger, usually consciously, but often unconsciously. To avoid the pain of parental disapproval the child will, usually unconsciously, stuff anger at that parent and pretend it doesn't exist. (Those of us who chose 100% opposition have a different set of problems to overcome.) In response to the parental pressure not to express the anger, that child may choose one or more of the following performance strategies: (1)give up all anger at everyone, (2)be critical of others' anger, (3)get angry with a younger sibling, (4)be weepy or depressed, (5)become isolated or withdrawn, (6)become angry at self or (7)displace rage on to classmates who are nerds or who have a different skin color. Later targets will be spouses, politicians, gays, African-Americans, etc. Please note how one simple-to-describe problem, denied anger at a parent, may result in a multiplicity of possible symptoms. Another subtle traumatic process often occurs when the child decides, consciously or unconsciously, to become just like a parent in one or more ways. Aspects of the child may be completely denied in the copying attempt. If this copying attempt is in any way based upon the hope that parent will give the child more love, acceptance or attention, then the copying behavior will probably be difficult to undo later.

This section's title, *Your Wish Is My Command*, accurately describes the feelings of most small children with respect to their parents. If the parent doesn't like a natural part of human existence (like sex, anger, tears, love or vulnerability), then the child will often attempt to please that parent by squelching those qualities.* As a result the child starts displaying many symptoms. This trauma is not so obvious as the trauma caused by an abusive parent. But it is trauma as defined earlier, "emotional shock producing a lasting effect on a person." The 97% of us growing up in dysfunctional families experienced this type of trauma shock (knot).

THE SEARCH FOR APPROVAL

Our childhood trauma knots propel us to act differently, to act for Mom and Dad in ways they want us to act, to win their approval to the maximum extent possible. We bend ourselves all out of shape in this search for approval and usually continue to do so well into adulthood. For those who never really examine themselves, this skewness may continue until their deaths.

Our continued search for parental approval leads to group-against-group belligerence in our culture today. "That group *should* approve of me (i.e., the way Mom and Dad *should* have approved of me); and if they don't, *they* must be in the wrong." My never-explored anger and grief (about my search for approval) drive my anger at targets of today. I fail to see that the real problem is my continued search as an adult for parental approval, a search started in childhood. If I am currently searching for others' approval, I have lost my personal *authenticity,* an essential ingredient of high self-esteem.

Searching for others' approval (i.e., performing for others) is insidious and incredibly widespread. Often our behavior is so automatic that we don't realize that if we followed our own real desires we would act very differently. Furthermore, we deny that we even have any negative feelings about such performing-for-others behavior.

Toilet Performance Routines. Most of us received training in washing our hands after using the toilet. One survey was done recently in a woman's rest room (by a woman in an out-of-the-way stall while keeping her feet well above the floor). The survey revealed that if women thought there was another person in the bathroom, 90% washed their hands. If they thought they were alone, 10% washed their hands. Would it be reasonable to conclude that most of the women in this survey group who washed their hands did so to make a favorable impression on others, instead of from a sense of personal authenticity?

Removing ourselves from the search for others' approval will yield many happiness dividends,* but it is one of life's more difficult growth tasks. (Despite many years of awareness, this author finds himself even today performing for others occasionally.)

Four Prisoners of Trauma
Words, Emotions, Sensations & Thoughts

UNTYING TRAUMA KNOTS

Two conditions increase our willingness to face our painful experiences: (1)As with my dog Pol, the presence of someone who cares (like a friend, spouse or therapist) may provide enough safety to face particularly fearful traumas, and (2)The ability to face trauma is improved by the lowering of defenses, as Pol's were lowered by the anesthesia. In humans, the lowering of defenses can also occur during hypnosis, in therapy, during addiction withdrawal, from lack of sleep and from lack of food.

> **Healing Tip.** To work on certain personal problems more effectively, with or without a paid therapist, try to create either or both of the conditions discussed above: increased safety and/or lower defenses. For example, a close friend might be willing to be there for you or you could fast for a few hours before attempting to start the work. I warn you, however, that close friends and spouses are suitable for some problems and absolutely wrong for others. If it feels right to you, try to enlist one of them for assistance. But I do not suggest investment either in their support or in the outcome of your attempt. For often we have such close people in our lives precisely because we have matching hangups. Just because you want to deal with a particular hangup or problem does not mean that they do. They may strongly resist any change.

If this trauma knot theory is correct, then therapies that tend to focus upon only one or two strands of the trauma knot might often prove ineffective in providing permanent relief. This is the case, for many therapies these days talk of "managing problems" or "managing anger" instead of resolving problems. The knowledge that trauma knots are of varying complexity and strengths can be useful in understanding why some symptoms are so persistent. Consider a woman with many similar experiences such as severe and mild abandonments over the course of her lifetime. For her, trauma knots associated with abandonment will probably be very resistant to loosening. Untying those abandonment knots entirely may seem impossible. Gaining insight (i.e., focusing on the *thinking* strand of the trauma knot) into the pattern of past abandonments may help make her aware of why she gets stressed when someone close to her goes away for a month. But this insight may do nothing to alleviate her stress. I call this "suffering smarter," but it is not my goal with my therapy clients.

LATER STRESS

Once we are traumatized, we carry the unresolved trauma with us forever, unless we can somehow get the trauma knot untied by therapy or another personal growth method. (Also, life experience will often untie many knots without significant effort on our parts.) If unresolved, the trauma typically shows up later in life as stress or numbing.

> **Specific Example of Later Sexual Stress.** For those sexually molested as children, sexuality carries with it large amounts of unhealthy stress during childhood. This stress typically carries over to adulthood. If sexual situations come into their adult lives, the unresolved sexual stresses are also immediately there waiting in the wings trying to get resolved. This is usually felt as tension and anxiety. To relieve this tension, sex frequently becomes an arena for acting out, either by circumscribing sexual behavior or by being promiscuous. Both these sexual strategies temporarily lower stress levels without helping to resolve the trauma. Other addictive behavior (such as drinking, smoking, overeating, etc.) can also be used to reduce the stress levels caused by sexual situations, similarly without lasting benefit in terms of resolving the trauma.*

Stress may appear later as bodily numbing, fear, anxiety, jumpiness, insomnia, panic or pain such as a headache or backache. (These are psychosomatic aches if caused by stress. Stress is a major factor in most such psychosomatic complaints.)

REDUCING/RESOLVING STRESS = THERAPY RESULT

There are many tools available for reducing or resolving stress. They cover the entire range of available therapies. Therapeutic methods of resolving and reducing stresses are discussed throughout this book: physically oriented methods in Chapters 5-7, how to change your thinking in Chapter 8, methods of emotional change in Chapters 9 & 10, and ways of changing spiritual beliefs in Chapter 11.

Therapy is defined (*Oxford*, 1980, s.v. "therapy") as "any treatment designed to relieve or cure an illness or disability." Symptoms of disability include bodily dysfunctions, emotional dysfunctions, thinking difficulties, spiritual belief difficulties, communication problems and undesirable behavior (all important therapy "stuff" discussed in the next few chapters). Because we are integrated beings, our dysfunctions are all interconnected. Therefore, the particular focus (on the body, mind, emotions or spirituality) of our chosen therapy is often not that important. Changing our thinking changes our emotions and vice versa. Similarly, freeing our body can free our communications or result in behavior change. The old idea that the kneebone is connected to the thighbone, which is connected to the hipbone, has strong parallels in terms of psychological disability. If one area of dysfunction changes, all areas are affected.**

ELEGANT SIMPLICITY OR SIMPLISTICALLY SIMPLE?

The trauma framework previously outlined is often initially considered by my therapist clients to be too simplistic. Their ideas usually change. *The rather simple trauma concept presented in this chapter explains much about psychology and therapy.*

---

* See Appendix A

** Possible additions to your I-WANT-LIST (see Appendix C):
  I want to act authentically.
  I want to face my traumas and move through them.

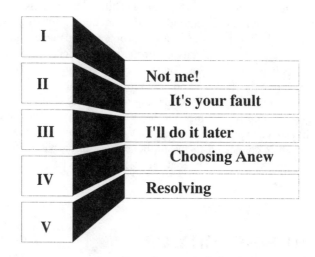

Stages of Growth & Healing

(It often happens that we are in Stage I for one of our problems and in Stage IV or V for the next.)

Chapter 4

Stages of Healing /
Making Changes

STAGES OF HEALING

<u>*STAGE I*</u> - **DENIAL** I deny that I have a problem. I just drink a few glasses of wine every day to soothe my nerves. I paste a smile on my face and pretend I am not bothered by my spouse, children, boss or parents. My mild depression seems normal and OK.

This stage is often confusing. Am I really in denial of a problem or is my lack of concern caused by the fact that I really don't have a problem? In either case, anger on your part will probably be unsuccessful in getting me to change. For if I am denying a real problem, my denial is already defensive. Anger by you then will often just make me more defensive and less willing to listen to you. If your anger is directed at my non-problem, your anger is just going to seem foolish to me. I am then likely to conclude that *you* are the one with a problem that needs solving.

<u>*STAGE II*</u> - **BLAME / HELPLESSNESS** I deny any fixable problem (i.e., fixable by me). I have a problem but there is nothing I can do about it; because it is all your fault, because I tried once to change it without success, because that is the way life is, because everyone is the same as me, etc. *But I do admit I have a problem.* This is often the stage of righteousness, judgments and anger that serve to keep me preoccupied with what I believe you should be doing rather than face my own discomfort. I often claim that it is impossible to change my unhappiness and anger until you change. If there is one stage that most represents the USA in the late 1980s and early 1990s, it is this stage. It seems as if each group is placing blame on outsiders for its problems and difficulties, thus dodging individual and collective responsibilities for changing group insiders. We have often convinced ourselves that others need to change

before happiness is possible for us. Suppose they never change? Are we then not locking ourselves into perpetual unhappiness? *The choice to be "happy" instead of "right" is frequently encountered and often difficult to make.* I believe this blaming righteous stage has been useful and necessary, for we have learned that anger and speaking out are OK. But I believe we will be harmed if we remain there much longer. It is also the unhappiest stage of healing.

STAGE III - **WAITING**   I have a *fixable* problem but choose to do nothing about it right now. This is a common resting point that we all *necessarily* choose every day for at least some of our problems.* We only can work on so many problems at once. The fewer the problems we choose to work on, the more likely will be our success at those fewer problems. *Waiting* does not necessarily deserve to be pejoratively labeled as procrastination, though such a label may occasionally be the truth. There is the need for occasional complete abstinence from "working on our problems" for a few days or weeks or even much longer.

STAGE IV - **WORKING** on my problem

  Stage IVa - Making a New Choice   It is essential to make a new choice such as: talk to my boss, parents, spouse or child in a new way, read a book on my problem (this book or one oriented to my specific problem), plan to record one's dreams, start a journal, meditate about the problem, try self-hypnosis, find a therapist, etc. Impulses need to be consulted, acknowledged and tried out (if they are not damaging). Most often the best new choice is just a small change to the previous choice.

  Stage IVb - Evaluating the New Choice   Do I still have the problem/symptoms? If yes, then I need to return to stage IVa to make a new choice or to stage III to let the problem rest for a time. My newer choice may just be a small modification if my earlier choice seemed to be along the right track. My newer choice will probably be very different if my earlier choice seemed to result in disaster.

  Stage V - **RESOLVING** (Letting That Old Problem Go). This is the stage where a particular problem or symptom finally seems small and no longer dominates me. Forgiveness, not the glib kind, is required here. Many "forgive" others falsely. When I dredge up or when I still feel strongly about old arguments/ actions, then I have not forgiven, and I have therapy/ growth work to do. Genuine forgiveness implies that not only do I fully understand why my parents (for example) intentionally or unintentionally traumatized me the way they did, but I fully understand my reactions and responses over the years. The words "if only" become meaningless, for I totally accept, without regrets, the problem (or symptom) and its history.

MAKING CHANGES IN SMALL STEPS
(*Stage IVa* above)

Many of us can read forever about the many ways we should make changes, but they are often particularly difficult to enact. How much easier it is to be a couch potato wolfing down unhealthy foods and beverages than to find the discipline to make some changes for our bodies' sake! More often than not, we are prone to make a grand gesture of change such as: "tomorrow I'll give up all alcohol forever and exercise for 90 minutes every day" without the awareness that those two major changes would take many months or years for even a highly disciplined person to accomplish. A few hours after we enact such an impossible program, we discard it like last New Year's resolutions. We can then blame (*Stage II*) our failure on advertising, agribusiness, the white male patriarchy, a hated political party, our abusive parents, etc. Or we can reinforce our own lack of self-esteem by considering ourselves a failure. Instead of blaming ourselves or others, it would be far healthier and more effective to self-talk along the lines of "I tried that and it didn't work - now I'll try something different" (*Stage IV*).

What works best in effecting personal changes is most often a series of small steps instead of a grand gesture attempting major sudden transformation. Remember how a baby starts to walk? A baby takes one very shaky step at a time accompanied by a big wide grin. One reason for the success of 12-Step programs like AA, Al-Anon and Overeater's Anonymous is that they emphasize one-day-at-a-time rather than a goal of "sobriety forever." Therefore, when you use this book, I suggest small steps, also the necessity for patience, self-compassion and <u>small</u> amounts of discipline.

"IMPOSSIBLE" SUCCESSES

An early question to ask yourself about your particular problem of concern is whether you would like to change. Do <u>not</u> at this stage ask yourself about whether such change is possible, for your response will probably be something like: "No, I can't change. That change is impossible. That is the way

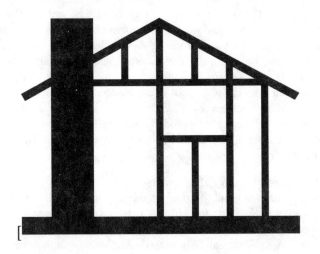

*Psychologically, most of us are
like structurally sound
fixer-upper houses that
have many potential repairs.*

I am. I always have been that way and I always will be that way." Just reiterating such an inflexible position will usually be enough to prevent all growth and change.

If you decide you do wish to change, then it is vital to realize that changes usually take time to accomplish. The long haul is frequently necessary. The right attitudes during this long haul are vital. Just because I want to change X does not mean that it is helpful to criticize myself or feel badly every time I do X. Instead, I need to keep my focus on the positive goal of Y (which I intend to replace X) and my possible next step along the road from X to Y. "What might I say or do or feel to move further along toward Y?" can be a very valuable question for myself to help me change. (Listen to your impulsive or intutive responses to that question.)

The more accepting I can be of myself during the process, the better the results I am likely to achieve. A loud "damn" or "I'm such a lousy person" rarely help to effect change.* Instead, if I can consciously come to believe that my problem behavior stems perfectly (see Chapter 8 for more on this perfection) from my entire life history, the happier I shall be. Also, I'll be more effective changing that behavior.

PROCRASTINATION

If you don't take action now but instead procrastinate, there is always a reason that is valid for you.* Perhaps the action itself or the timing of the action is wrong for you, perhaps you need to grow before the action may be accomplished, or perhaps you just need to overcome inertia. Whatever the case, there is likely to be some fear that needs to be faced. If your inertia stems from fear, can you overcome your fear of this specific change by modifying your beliefs? Do you fear all changes?

The best course when faced with procrastination is often to do the first step of the action anyway. If the first step goes well, inertia was probably the cause of your procrastination. If you try the first step and it goes badly, then procrastination is probably right for you now; and you will probably need to examine yourself further. Also, be on the lookout for self-deception concerning procrastination, because addictions (such as TV, food, smoking, etc.) are often used to deceive ourselves in these matters.

When faced with a multistage process such as a complete change in career or an attempt to start up a business, always keep yourself as current as possible with actions. If you know, for example, that one of your next steps is to find out what city permits you need for your new business, this small unfinished task will <u>add to your current level of stress</u>. Most people do not realize that a simple unfinished task such as gathering a piece of information can increase our stress levels.

> *Our intentions to read 100 books or do 25 projects around the house rob us of present day energy. Instead, turn such intentions in your mind into <u>possibilities</u>, as suggested in Appendix C.*

If you intend action, your body feels the anticipation until you take the action or you change your intention. It is easiest to change these intentions into possibilities. You can review these possibilities every month, to select those to be attempted next month.

In a multistage change process that can take months or years, there will be times when no action is appropriate. At such times procrastination is not the issue, and it is important then not to be self-critical.

A PERSONAL EXAMPLE

Recently as I have been writing and rewriting drafts of this book, my lack of aerobic exercise started to enter my awareness frequently. My thoughts were: "But that is the way I am as I write this book. That is not a problem for me now." In retrospect, this was obviously *Stage I-Denial*, but it felt reasonable and made sense to me because I have had to drop so much else from my life to concentrate on writing. Then one day recently I witnessed a teenager beside me at a bus-stop explode instantaneously from quiet stillness to a full running mode. This explosion was the start of a successful chase of another bus suddenly spotted several blocks away. Being a witness to that scene triggered my awareness that it wasn't exercise I was missing, just aerobic exercise. My thoughts were: "That's interesting, but I can't do anything about that. That is the way I am." This was *Stage II - Blame/ Helplessness*, claiming that my problem was not solvable by me. Allowing a little "maybe it is solvable" into consciousness propelled me to *Stage IV*. I did not need to *wait* in *Stage III*, because I could immediately attempt a new *Stage IV* choice. The new choice I made was to choose to examine why I could exercise (2-3 miles a day walking) but was unable to get aerobic exercise. The images and thoughts that came to mind were about my infancy and the pain I learned then to associate with large bodily movements (i.e., movements of large muscle groups enough to cause sweating/ overheating).

During my infancy, from three to six months of age, I was often placed during summer days in a very hot room, too hot for an infant. My parents zealously followed a predetermined schedule. Therefore, I stopped my crying responses because they were ineffective, and I stopped my large bodily movements because they just brought me more discomfort in the excessive heat.

I now faced a new adult choice, either to feel the infant feelings that were still locked up in my trauma knots gained that long ago summer or to explore another method of healing. Because I had often explored similar issues before, the predominant feelings of infant rage and infant grief took only a few minutes to emerge and to dissipate. I then could aerobically exercise for the first time in several weeks. *Stage IVb - Evaluation:* so far so good. *Stage V - Resolving* will only be real and lasting when all my infant-aerobics-fear is gone for good. I know, as I write these words, that so far I have not felt the urge to grieve the lost years of being stuck in that way. Once that grief arises, I am confident that I shall feel my way through it rapidly, but until then I am in *Stage III - Waiting*.

Also, I may have more difficulties with this issue ahead of me that may require more new choices, more new-to-me feelings and more changes in my thinking. (How prophetic! Now several months after writing the above, more difficulties have emerged concerning getting aerobic exercise permanently into my life. More new *Stage IV choices* are clearly ahead for me.)

CHANGING OTHERS EFFECTIVELY

We could accomplish wondrous changes in the world around us if only each of us would follow the maxim: "Think globally and act locally." One valid not-so-obvious meaning of those words is that I cannot have a changed world unless I change. I need to heal where I am unhealthy and unhappy even if all those bigots, chauvinists, ripoff businesses and sleazy politicians change not one iota.

Local action is also much more effective than it might appear at first glance. It doesn't seem as if my one telephone call to my senator makes much difference. But when all the calls are added up in the senator's office, it does. (Most important is the sense of *personal* satisfaction from voicing an opinion instead of doing nothing.) There were no demonstrations condemning a recent attorney general nomination; instead, senators received thousands of clearheaded phone calls opposing the nomination. The nomination was promptly scuttled.

"I object," "I oppose" and "That feels wrong" (spoken in calm tones without anger) are three powerful assertive statements that are effective in influencing others. Outrage, calling someone names and negative judgments are, by comparison, ineffective because they typically evoke a defensive response. Getting the opposition defensive often just hardens their position and makes them more resistant to change. Therefore, in your local actions, you will be most effective if you are assertive, not condemning. Blow off steam with your friends (or with your therapist), but for maximum effectiveness be calmly assertive with your opposition, your senator and those whom you would like to change.**

At times all of us do nothing. "My efforts would make no difference" is frequently the reasoning behind the inaction. "That is not my responsibility" is another favorite dodge. If something global (or more local) strongly energizes you, you are a part of it. Take some action: make a phone call, write a note or talk with a friend. The decision about how much action is appropriate for you will always be with you, and some trial-and-error process will normally be necessary to figure out your correct level of activity. There are those who would strongly argue that if you have continued negative energy concerning a problem, you are now part of the problem. Taking no action keeps you negatively energized and does nothing to change the global problem.

A LOUSY WAY OF MAKING CHANGES = SELF CRITICISM

One common response to our upsets is self-criticism such as, "I shouldn't get upset at that Situation A." This response inhibits change, for it denies the inherent logic of our upset responses and usually prevents a careful look at our reasons for getting upset.

If you get upset at your partner's leaving off the toothpaste cap, there is logic and reasoning going on within you that is valid for you now! Of course you get upset at that. We always get upset for reasons specific to us. The goal is often to change our thinking so that we feel fine (and not upset) when Situation A occurs again (more in Chapter 8). Self-flagellation does not help us attain this goal.

Rx: *The logic (the reasons for our upsets in Situation A) is what we often need to explore and change. If completely successful, then we will feel fine when Situation A recurs. This is* **_resolution_**.

* See Appendix A

**Possible additions to your I-WANT-LIST (see Appendix C):
  I want to make some new choices concerning my problem with _____.
  I want to look for local action that I can accomplish concerning my problem with _____.

*What about the joyful positive
side of living in a body
that works well, able to express
love and who you are?*

Chapter 5

Your Body Is
Not A Carcass

IGNORE YOUR BODY,
SUFFER THE CONSEQUENCES

Do you routinely ignore your body and its signals, as you might ignore a carcass alongside the highway? Is your body dull and lifeless, like a carcass? If so, you may be like many psychotherapy clients who have the mistaken impression that just doing verbal psychotherapy will eventually make them happy. What they overlook is that much of their emotional unhappiness stems from a dysfunctional body which is itself struggling to overcome the effects of smoking, drinking, being a couch potato, an unhealthy diet, extra pounds, addictive food allergy, etc. Because our emotional happiness is so interconnected with bodily health, ease and comfort, few of us will experience emotional happiness and contentment if we neglect our bodies.*

Many of us are badly out of touch with our physical bodies. When we were young, we made the unconscious choice not to feel certain parts or all of our bodies. This was preferable to feeling the pain associated with traumatic events in our lives. What made it painful to have our bodies were all the parental and societal messages that squelched us. They caused us (1)to stuff our anger and hatred, (2)to conceal and deny our sexuality, (3)to eat our words, (4)to overeat to please Mommy, (5)to act like a big girl/boy by not crying, (6)to act invisible to avoid abuse, (7)to feel badly about being small and weak and (8)etc. It wasn't just the words and emotions that got stuffed. Because we are interconnected organisms, if we shut down our words and emotions, our bodies also shut down.* Numbness as a child was preferable to pain.

Be in the Moment Exercise. Try for two minutes to be as fully aware of your body as possible, (the feelings in your arm, your torso, the itch {scratch it if you like}, the sensations in your feet, etc. The purposes for such an exercise are (1)to regain body awareness and (2)to live with more awareness in the present moment. (We tend to be stuck worrying about the future or ruminating about the past.) *One common feature of those who are happy is their ability to spend most of their time in the present moment.** Therefore, it behooves us all to develop that skill, feeling in the present moment, thinking about the present moment and being in the present moment as fully as possible.

In verbal talk therapy so much energy is typically invested in talking, thinking and emoting that the body is frequently overlooked. Yet healing methods that focus primarily on the body are sometimes easier and quicker than other means of healing. Commonly too, they promote positive unexpected emotional benefits. One particularly useful goal to have in life is to be completely comfortable with your body. This may, of course, require that you find some therapy.

BODYWORK THERAPY

There are many bodywork therapies available to help heal and free the body. I personally have tried a few of these methods. Based upon my experiences I don't have a specific type to recommend, but instead some general comments. Most bodywork therapies attempt gently or more forcefully (ask any potential practitioners whether their methods are gentle or more forceful) to change your body by physical manipulation in the direction of enhanced well-being and wholeness. This manipulation is an attempt to eliminate physical and/or psychological problems that manifest in the body as stiffness, dullness, coolness, misalignment, lifelessness or muscle knots. They are usually successful in the short run. The result often feels great!

Unfortunately, such changes often do not last because the bodywork only loosened the associated trauma knots. To untie these knots sufficiently it has been my experience that bodywork therapies also often need to incorporate words and emotions in addition to bodily manipulation.* My opinion is that one needs to deliberately seek after and elicit words and emotions for such bodywork therapies to be lastingly effective.

There are some bodywork practitioners who would say that such short term bodily changes showed the need for more body therapy so that your body would "learn" over time the right way to be. My experience suggests that this learning sometimes happens and sometimes does not. When it doesn't, the consumer spends extra money without satisfactory results. This is a trap for some bodywork therapists and clients: they need to keep returning for more bodywork. Otherwise, the evidence of their trauma knots (i.e., muscle knots, stiffness, pain, etc.) returns. Just because I have pointed out a possible trap for some practitioners does not mean that most are so ensnared. There are many available bodyworkers who regularly and routinely *elicit the words and emotions that will help to permanently loosen trauma knots.* If you are considering a particular bodyworker, I suggest that you ask about this issue.

If the idea of bodywork appeals to you, I do recommend it. Compared with conventional talk therapy, bodywork is often less expensive, since most bodywork therapies last a few weeks instead of many months. For someone who is uncomfortable about being touched, the experience of just one session will often have lasting value. For someone whose trauma shows up as many physical symptoms, such work can be particularly valuable. Many can benefit immensely just by becoming more aware of their bodies.

Finally, while erotic massage might not be considered "professional" bodywork, such an experience can have permanent lasting value for those who have tended to deny or reject aspects of their sexuality. If nothing else, erotic massage can feel wonderful, whether or not it is done by a significant other.

BE YOUR OWN BODYWORKER

While I know of no "official" bodywork that talks of doing it by and for yourself, there is one body-changing possibility that could well prove as successful as hiring a professional bodyworker. Instead of having to continue to go back to a bodyworker to cement the gains of the bodywork, this method teaches you to do that process yourself.

The method I suggest is described in Egoscue's *The Egoscue Method of Health Through Motion.* By following his directions for self-diagnosis of dysfunction followed by exercises designed for that dysfunction, you can realign and shape your body into its optimal form and function. He emphasizes that our bodies usually get dysfunctional through disuse of our muscular-skeletal system, whose design craves much more motion than we give it in today's technological society. He suggests very strongly that many sports-related and work-related injuries such as shin splints, carpal-tunnel syndrome and tennis elbow are caused by poor alignment of our bodies before and during those activities not by the activities themselves. If you have any pain anywhere in your muscular-skeletal system, I recommend that you find and read this book, as it shatters popular myths about our bodies. (Also, if your toes are not directly in front of your ankles when walking or if your shoulders and head tend to droop forward, read Egoscue's book. For you are a prime candidate for significant avoidable future bodily pain.)

The one significant ingredient likely to be missing from such a self-help method is the emotion associated with bodily trauma. For some, such an omission is not that important, because many bodily dysfunctions are just habits and may not have a significant emotional trauma component.

If emotional trauma is present, changing the body to its proper form by way of Egoscue's exercises will make the emotions more accessible. Unraveling and straightening the dysfunctional body is the same as loosening a strand of a trauma knot. The emotions and words (the other usual strands in the trauma knot that also need unraveling) can then be more readily expressed while doing the exercises or during some talk therapy with a therapist.

TOUCHING AND BEING TOUCHED

What happens when we meet a new friendly dog or cat? We tend to stroke the animal, using our hands on its body. What usually happens when we meet a new friendly person? Beyond a perfunctory handshake, we avoid touching. Why the difference? What would it be like to stroke a newly met person for the length of time one might stroke a newly met dog? What would such strokes look like? Our reluctance to touch stems from ingrained cultural training that such touching would be considered sexual in nature. Yet we all have seen films of our ape cousins grooming each other for hours without a trace of evident lust.

> **Growth Tip.** Fantasize (or visualize) for a few moments meeting a new person and stroking that person's body as you would a newly met friendly cat or dog. How does that feel? Is it OK with you? (I am not suggesting you do this to a stranger.) Fantasize doing that often to a spouse/ significant-other when they end their workday. Do you want them to reciprocate?

Men, seemingly more than women, have been adversely affected by the cultural prohibition against touch, particularly the prohibition against touching another man. It is a significant growth experience for many men to finally find the courage to hug another man for the first time, discovering that there can be emotional caring without sexual feelings.*

Do you touch enough? Under what circumstances and with whom do you want more? What is stopping you from touching and being touched more often? Our society historically has touched far too little. One of the many reasons why the crime of sexual abuse occurs so often is that adult perpetrators are trying to compensate for lack of childhood or present-day touch. It has been said that we all need 8-12 meaningful touches a day. Are you giving and receiving that amount or more?

AVOIDING TOXINS

It is common sense that we need to minimize toxins, for we do not tolerate them well. Common toxins can take many forms: toxins in or on our foods, toxins in our homes, people and relationships who are toxic, toxic ideas and the toxic effects of lack of exercise.

While there has been much emphasis on food toxins, it would be beneficial if there were similar emphasis on other toxins. We all learned not to drink the chemicals in the containers under our sinks, but what about the vapors from those chemicals? How about the vapors from the garden, painting and house-repair chemicals in our basements and garages? We spend billions cleaning up toxins miles away from us, yet we typically do nothing about similar items in our own homes. Common home toxins have been found to cause many negative bodily reactions, not just for children who might ingest them, but also for many who inhale vapors. For toxins our defenses are like water dikes; once they start to leak, they start leaking more and more. Therefore, *it is our total toxin load over our entire lifetimes that is relevant*, not just whether we are currently showing negative symptoms. I shall discuss toxic people, relationships, emotions and ideas in more detail throughout the book. While some people automatically consider some "negative" feelings and emotions to be toxic, I believe that only those that don't go away are toxic (see Chapter 9).

*If Anything Is
Sacred, the Human
Body Is Sacred.*

Walt Whitman

The toxic effects on our bodies caused by lack of physical play are often discounted and ignored. Being a couch potato shifts body chemistry in unhealthy ways, destroys muscle mass, causes depression and "yuckiness" and makes us more receptive to diseases.

COUCH POTATO BENEFITS

There are several benefits(?) that accrue to those of us who decide that being an immobile couch potato is the route we shall follow:

(1)We cherish our 43 extra pounds. We relish being droopy and draggy, without much energy.

(2)We come to enjoy firsthand, up close and personally, more cancer operations, heart bypasses and other modern day medical miracles.

(3)Because of being overweight, we become sexually irresistible to others. The quality and quantity of our sex lives know no bounds.

(4)We can avoid *feeling, thinking and loving.*

(5)We gain the opportunity to die early.

What wonderful benefits!

PSYCHOLOGICAL REASONS WHY WE DON'T EXERCISE

There is not likely to be one psychological reason you avoid physical play (i.e., exercise). Instead, there are many possible reasons, which may require some change on your part if physical play is to be a regular, routine part of your life. Psychological (sometimes unconscious) causes often are:

(1)I am following in a parent's footsteps. That parent was sedentary and believed vigorous exercise was not OK. Me too.

(2)I need to shut down parts of my body because of trauma. Structured exercising or physical play would trigger trauma buttons that I wish to avoid. I learned as an infant or young child that my body is not OK.

(3)I believe I am weak (most of us have this kid belief within us to some degree). Therefore, I prove it today by being weak as a result of not exercising.

(4)I believe competition is bad so I avoid exercise. I do not realize that my labeling competition as bad is part of *my* difficulty.

(5)By avoiding exercise, I gain weight, which feels like added *protection* against an "unsafe" world.

(6)I have been traumatized to believe that it is not OK to feel good, so I feel "yucky" all the time by not exercising.

(7)If as a child I was traumatized to be inactive, rigid or passive, then vigorous activities may feel dangerous (though I may hide the fear from myself and give myself another rationale).

The above list is certainly incomplete. I suggest that you create your own. It will likely be productive for you in making your life more vigorous.

FITNESS IN 30 MINUTES A WEEK?

I highly recommend the book titled *Total Fitness in 30 Minutes a Week* by Laurence E. Morehouse Ph.D. and Leonard Gross. Surely you have noted that most books written about exercise are written for athletes or for those who want maximum health? "You must exercise for the length of time specified to obtain maximum cardiovascular fitness" is a typical statement to be found in such volumes. But who wants maximum cardiovascular fitness at such a cost? It takes much willpower to spend a total of three hours a week exercising. Such is a typical amount of time suggested by many of these books. The vast majority of people attempting such a routine will soon quit because it just takes too much discipline.

Instead, I suggest the program devised by Dr. Morehouse, then professor of exercise physiology at UCLA and creator of the original exercise program for USA space astronauts. His 1975 book outlines a program whose goal is a reasonable, not maximum, level of fitness. Not surprisingly, Dr. Morehouse was criticized by colleagues who felt maximum physical fitness or maximum cardiovascular fitness "should" be the goal. However, what those colleagues failed to realize was that those whom Dr. Morehouse was attempting to reach would usually fail any approach that was significantly more rigorous.

Dr. Morehouse (Morehouse and Gross 1976, 17) instantly revealed the audience he was trying to reach with his first words: "I hate to exercise."

His initial program provides for: stretching, strengthening of muscle groups and moderate aerobics - all accomplished in 30 minutes a week* (ten minutes of exercise three times a week). Those of you who follow the latest trends in successful weight-loss will no doubt note that this program meets two requirements of successful weight-loss programs: (1)aerobics and (2)muscle strengthening.

Do look for this classic book in your used bookstore and follow its recommendations. Reasonable fitnessis the best goal for most of us.

AN EXERCISE PROGRAM FOR THOSE WHO HATE TO EXERCISE

Moderation is always the goal initially. Speak with your doctor first if you have not been exercising regularly or if you have some physical difficulty that might preclude exercising.

Dr. Morehouse recommends one minute of limbering and stretching. His four recommended stretching exercises require moderate amounts of reaching, twisting, and bending and are to be done in a "leisurely languid manner." You can create your own limbering and stretching exercises, follow Dr. Morehouse's, or find another book with similar suggested exercises.

Your aerobic exercises may also be different from Dr. Morehouse's, yet accomplish similar results. For the upper body, possibilities include using hand weights (soup cans will do while simultaneously exercising the lower body), or a treadmill with moving arm handles. For lower body development, possibilities include: aerobic walking or jogging, a treadmill, a stair-stepper, or other aerobic exercise/device (preferably low-impact). If Dr. Morehouse's book is unavailable, then I recommend reading others of the genre in your local library if you wish more detailed information about pulse rates, interval training, stretching, endurance, etc. But remember, *reasonable fitness* is the best goal for most of us.

The most important step is the first. After checking with your doctor, start moderate exercising for ten minutes three times a week. Do what feels best for you, as much as possible within the framework described in the preceding paragraphs. The keys are: (1)to do it regularly for development of some muscle strengthening, which *will* happen if the upper and lower bodies are exercised moderately 30 minutes a week, and (2)to exercise at a moderate heart rate. The key is to get started doing something regularly. Fine-tuned adjustments can wait for later.

> **Success Tip.** You will be more likely to succeed if you give yourself concrete praise every time you exercise (for more about rewarding yourself, see Appendix E). For example, place on an obvious shelf a symbol of completed exercise. A penny will do. Just place a penny on a highly visible kitchen shelf every time you exercise during the week. This will jog your memory and serve as a bit of important praise for you every time you see that shelf. This can work with stones, shells, glasses, refrigerator magnets, pencils or whatever you choose in whatever location seems best for you: refrigerator door, kitchen shelf, TV or table. (Do not use the ineffective method where you set up three pennies at the beginning of the week and remove one penny from view each time you exercise. Also, do not use food as a reward.) This success tip is highly effective, more so than one would think. Try it!

AWAKENING AND REVITALIZING THE BODILY SENSES

Is your hearing dulled and closed down, causing you to miss the bird's warbling? Do you seem to have tunnel vision, thus overlooking the sparkle of the visual details around you? Have you really tasted and smelled a lemon recently? Do you *customarily* feel sensual pleasure in the heat or cold of your surroundings?

Most of us have dulled our senses. To invigorate them may require therapy, but not necessarily. I recommend that you practice some of Dr. Fezler's images found in *Creative Imagery*, a book that I also recommended in Chapter 2 for the development of sparkle. His images will also strongly promote the awakening and revitalization of the bodily senses.**

> **Celebrating.** *Say the following aloud with feeling.* I appreciate the health my body does have. I am grateful for my taste, smell, touch, hearing and sight abilities. I appreciate _____ (you fill the blank).

*For maximum happiness,
most of us need to
savor, enjoy, and respect
our bodies more.*

---

*   See Appendix A

** Possible Additions to your I-WANT-LIST (see Appendix C): (Reminder: no more than 3-4
    I-Wants)
    I want to try some bodywork.
    I want to do my own bodywork, following the principles of *The Egoscue Method of
       Health Though Motion.*
    I want to exercise 3X a week, 10 minutes each time.
    I want to obtain the book titled *Total Fitness in 30 Minutes a Week.*
    I want to awaken my senses: hearing, sight, smell, taste and touch.
    I want to obtain the book titled *Creative Imagery.*
    I want to be completely comfortable with my physical body.

Celebration Time

Thirty years ago most doctors would have been horrified that you and I might be testing ourselves for food allergies. It is time to celebrate how much they have changed in the past years. Today, most doctors have broken the bonds of "doctor always knows best" and "whatever involves injections, pills or surgery must be the right thing to do". These changes on their parts and our willingness to assume more responsibility for our health bode well for a much healthier society in the future.

Chapter 6

Mystery Meat

ARE ANY OF THESE PROBLEMS YOURS?

Depressed	Alcohol	Irritable
Overweight	Uncontrolled Angry Outbursts	Tense
Compulsive Eating	Headaches	Schizophrenia
Insomnia	Hyperactive	Anxious
Learning Problems	Confused	Asthma
Blurred Vision	Night Sweats	Nervous Stomach
Adult Acne	Fatigue	Poor Memory

IS MYSTERY MEAT YOUR PROBLEM?

Do you remember that strange meat-loaf-like dish they always served at Thursday lunch in school and military cafeterias? To disguise it further, it was usually smothered in metallic tasting gravy. Most referred to this dish as mystery meat. I am not suggesting your current problems were caused by being allergic to that gourmand's delight. Instead, I am disguising this section hoping to whet your curiosity so that your reaction will <u>not</u> be to skip this chapter. For the problem I intend to discuss, the truth <u>is</u> usually a mystery. Allergies *sneakingly* cause many symptoms that are commonly classified as therapy symptoms, including <u>all</u> those listed in the above paragraph.* (Of course, allergies are not the only possible cause of the above symptoms.)

The Three
Most Common
Villains

Corn   Dairy   Wheat

Are they causing <u>your</u>
"psychological" problems?

It may be surprising to learn that many, if not most of our food allergies, are a total mystery to us. This goes against the common idea that whatever I am allergic to will give me a big rash, hives or other dramatic reactions after every exposure. This common idea about allergies describes one variety of food allergy, fixed allergy (though our bad reactions may not be dramatic). If our reactions to an offending food are strong only if we have recently eaten too much of it, then this suggests a cyclic allergy. Usually, we know our fixed and cyclic food allergies.

Addictive allergies, however, are often a mystery. They are nevertheless very real. What are addictive allergies? The following quotation is from *Five Day Allergy Relief System* (Mandell and Scanlon 1980, 37):

> You may have a type of allergy in which you eat the same foods quite frequently and have developed an allergic type of addiction (an *addictive* allergy). Most people with food addiction are completely unaware that this process is taking place in their body. If an addicted person misses a meal that would normally include the food to which he is allergic, *allergic-addictive* withdrawal symptoms appear. To avoid the discomfort of a withdrawal reaction, a person has to keep eating the food to which he is allergic to stave off withdrawal symptoms. Dr. Rinkel described this blocking phenomenon, where the appearance of symptoms is prevented by the repeated exposures to the offending substance, as *masking*.*

So why bother learning about such allergies if the withdrawal symptoms are not apparent? Although withdrawal symptoms may be masked, other symptoms resulting from continued eating of such foods could be what you consider your most significant *psychological* symptoms!

The list at the beginning of this chapter is a Pandora's box of problems typically considered the province of therapists. Of course, there is no guarantee that addictive food allergies are causing your problem(s) on that list, but isn't it worth your time and energy to find out? People like you and me unknowingly waste time and money on therapists/doctors for relief of these problems.

COMMON FOOD ALLERGIES

The most common food allergies are dairy and wheat (with corn not far behind). When testing, carefully check labels for dairy, wheat and corn, (and their less obvious appearances as whey, syrup, bran, etc.). These three most common offenders are found in a wide array of foods. Additionally, any other foods that you regularly consume, or for which you have cravings, are likely culprits. Dr. Mandell states that "over the past twenty-five years, my colleagues and I have found that

wheat	potatoes	chicken
corn	pork	lettuce
coffee	oranges	soy products
cane sugar	carrots	peanuts
milk	tomatoes	green beans
eggs	yeast	oats
beef	apples	chocolate

are prominent among the foods that often cause allergic reactions in our patients" (Mandell and Scanlon 1980, 115). The above listed foods have become overly important to our diets, both in their plain forms and also in their combined forms. Because of such high levels of ingestion, many people have become highly allergic to these foods.

WHAT TEST FOR FOOD ALLERGIES?

If you have one of the difficulties on the list at this chapter's beginning, then I suggest that you test yourself for a possible addictive food allergy. I am not suggesting that you get an old-style medical test for allergies. Those tests have proved to be inaccurate.

Testing your *blood* for allergic reactions will yield false results. This is because your body in real life reacts not to the food itself, but to what passes through digestive walls. For example, if a specific food is made of chemicals I J K & L, the digestive process will change some of those chemicals. What is then absorbed through digestive walls and eventually into the blood may be chemicals I J O & P. Absorbed chemicals/foods are what cause allergic reactions, not chemicals K & L, for example, which never get absorbed. Thus, blood tests are often inaccurate. So too are the old-style scratch tests. They depend upon the body developing a special blood *reagin* which will cause the redness in a scratch test. Reagins are not always developed. Therefore, the scratch test is also notoriously inaccurate. There are some reliable allergy tests that are now available, under-the-tongue and inhalation tests among others. I suggest that you be an informed medical consumer and ask your physician about the reliability of whatever allergy testing is being done.

DOING THE TESTING YOURSELF

Actually, the testing you do on yourself** for food allergy will be the most accurate of all, if done carefully. Why? Because when you test yourself by eating your suspected foods, your individual unique absorption and digestive processes are part of the test. Your bodily reactions will tell you explicitly if that food is good or bad for you.

Foods rarely eaten such as pomegranates and pigs' livers are unlikely to be addictive allergy problems. It is those foods you often crave or are regularly in your diet that are the ones to which you are most often addictively allergic.

Testing for addictive food allergy is not that hard.* See Appendix D for instructions if you do not have Dr. Mandell's book available. You have nothing to lose except possibly a few of your worst "psychological" problems. (See the beginning of this chapter for the list of these "psychological" problems that have at times been caused <u>solely</u> by allergies.) **TEST YOURSELF ASAP!**

This author hopes you now understand
the truth written on this button:

* See Appendix A

**Possible additions to your I-WANT-LIST (see Appendix C):
      I want to test myself for food allergies.
      I want to read Dr. Mandell's *5-Day Allergy Relief System.*

This woman finally obtained enough love, sex and human touch in her life. Her excess pounds then melted away without effort.

Chapter 7

DIETING IMPULSES OFTEN LEAD TO BLIND ALLEYS

Being overweight is usually a particularly difficult problem to overcome, because its causes are typically complex. Known causes include the physical, the biochemical, emotional difficulties and ingrained habit patterns. The typical first impulse of those attempting to solve a weight problem is to start a diet, the newer the diet the better. This almost never works permanently. While weight is usually able to be removed by dieting, it rarely stays off, because its causes have not been eliminated.

Instead of dieting, your most productive first impulse might be to examine your fitness. If <u>your</u> triathlon is a stroll from the couch to the cupboard to the refrigerator and back, any diet you attempt that excludes exercise will probably fail.* You probably skipped over the earlier chapter on how to obtain a reasonable level of fitness. Can I convince you to go back and read it carefully? It really is <u>not</u> a physical fitness regimen devised by your sadistic old high school gym coach. Please! I am not talking hours and hours of drudgery at a sweaty health club, rather a total of about thirty minutes a week. Please do read and understand the fitness section in Chapter 5. It is worth reading!

If the speed of your metabolism rivals that of a slow lumbering elephant, then your shape will also likely resemble the elephant. You <u>can</u> change your metabolism with a moderate amount of exercise.* There is today wide agreement among weight control experts that Covert Bailey expressed an important truth about the choice facing overweight people when he titled his book *Fit Or Fat*. Without the choice of a <u>moderate</u> level of fitness, continued fatness is almost a sure thing for those who are overweight.

Did you also skip over the last chapter on allergies? Many food allergies are <u>not</u> obvious. They stress our bodies without our awareness and we tend to become addicted to (i.e., wolf down frequently) precisely those foods to which we are allergic. If you have unknown addictive food allergies, it is a significant possibility that no diet will work. Nor will any other means of losing weight work, other than removing from your diet the foods to which you are allergic. Discovering your own food allergies could well produce significant weight loss for you with essentially <u>no ongoing effort</u> other than to avoid foods to which you are allergic. Doesn't that sound heavenly? You might want to read Appendix D to learn how this author lost weight and thigh-inches permanently in a very short time (days!). Lost weight and thigh-inches might be a permanent part of your future too, if you discover and eliminate foods to which you have an addictive allergy.

The emptiness in our lives today causes billions of our unwanted pounds. If I am not giving or receiving enough emotional love, I am likely to try to compensate for love-emptiness with food-fullness. Similarly, I am likely to try to compensate for lack of human touch or sex by trying to make myself feel better through food intake. If love, sex or touch is missing from your life, what are your plans for changing the situation? Your excess weight will probably be difficult to lose without enough love, sex and touch in your life.

ADD-A-CARROT DIET

Is it possible that consistent moderate weight loss could reliably result from a diet as simple as eating more carrots? Yes!

The basic rule of this diet is to add a carrot (varied with other low calorie "rabbit-food") *at or near the beginning of* every meal. Why should this work? This works because a bulky carrot at or near the meal's beginning leaves no room in the stomach at the meal's end for the extra ice-cream or cheesecake. That saves perhaps 500 calories a day, which translates to a weight loss of about a pound a week.

The same result could be obtained by consuming any other low-calorie vegetable, singly or in combination: radishes, cucumbers, turnips, jicama, zucchini, tomatoes, celery, mushrooms, dill pickles, etc. Low-calorie vegetable juices from your own juicer or from the market would also produce the same results. Soup is another possibility, provided it is low-calorie, like a consomme. Even plain water at the beginning of a meal will tend to create a full feeling in the stomach sooner in the meal. This will reduce the amount of food consumed at the end.

Getting Started on Your Add-A-Carrot Diet. (1)Stock up on low-calorie food items, avoiding those specific foods, perhaps broccoli, which you remember Mom trying hard to get you to eat, and (2)Create a reward system for yourself, perhaps small shells on a kitchen shelf, such that a new shell appears on that shelf every time you eat a bulky low-calorie food at or near the beginning of a meal. (For more about rewards, see Appendix E.) At the end of a week, count the number of shells.

This add-a-carrot diet will <u>not</u> work if psychological problems, lack of exercise or addictive food allergies cause your overweight difficulties. It likely <u>will</u> be effective if your extra pounds are primarily the result of poor habits.You have nothing to lose, however, from the attempt at such a diet. An added benefit is that this diet can help to change your eating patterns in the direction of lower-fat, higher-fiber food items. Most overweight people have high-fat eating patterns that need changing no matter what else causes their overweight conditions.

CHANGING OUR FOOD PREFERENCES

We commonly tend to think the reason we eat a particular food regularly is that we like it. A more accurate statement would be that we like that food <u>because</u> we eat it regularly. This is an important difference, because the more accurate statement leads to many possibilities for changing from a fattening diet to one that is slimming. If I have no psychological trauma or allergy associated with a particular healthy food, eating it regularly will cause me to start liking it more.*

Millions of us have experienced the change from regular milk to blue (nonfat) milk. Initially the blue variety tasted thin and watery, and we missed the "right-tasting" regular milk. After a few weeks, however, it was the blue variety that tasted right; and the regular milk then seemed too thick, almost like cream. <u>We came to prefer what we ate regularly.</u>**

This is often a basic success principle involved in weight-loss programs. <u>Their</u> food is eaten for weeks or months, food lower in fat and higher in fiber. At the end of the program, your food preferences have changed! You can use this principle for yourself and by yourself. Following the above Add-A-Carrot diet for a month will do just that, change your food preferences. If you want to increase your liking of healthy foods, then get them into your diet regularly in the easiest way possible for you. Cook up rice, divide it into seven

*How many of his extra
pounds would disappear if
he changed his food
preferences?*

or more small portions and reheat it throughout the next week in your microwave. Do the same with beans, soup, winter squash or whatever healthy food you wish to make a more significant part of your diet. (Success may not result if you attempt this with foods that were forced upon you as a child.)

> **Food Exercise.** For your next meal or meals, try to stay completely focused upon the acts of eating, sensations, tastes, aromas, textures, feelings, etc. This exercise serves two purposes: (1)it will help bring you more often into the present moment, which will make you feel more contented no matter what and (2)it will probably help with weight control, for one important feature of many successful weight loss plans is their requirement that you become more *aware* of the process of eating.

If you are a parent who wants to change your child's eating in a healthier direction, provide a reward (longer story-time, TV-time or whatever) for eating a tablespoon of everything served. Your child will come to like almost everything that is regularly served.

> **Success Tip - Flavor Instead of Fat**.** An ingrained habit pattern in this culture is the widespread consumption of too much fat. Yet when we attempt to reduce the fat, we often don't feel satisfied with the food consumed. To feel satisfied with reduced fat items, it is helpful to replace the fat with flavor. If I use nothing on my green beans, I may feel deprived and unsatisfied. If I substitute garlic salt and lemon juice instead of butter, I feel satisfied "because the beans are interesting." Setting up your own flavor substitution goals could be productive. For example, if you like the combination of garlic and onion, you might set up a goal of having garlic powder and onion flakes on three vegetables during the next week. Vary this in the following weeks to include: other spices, lemon juice, low-salt soy sauce, poppy seeds, salsa or other new-to-you flavors.

ARE YOUR EXTRA POUNDS PSYCHOLOGICAL?

Much of the time the causes of excess weight are unclear. Books that deal with the issue from a habit perspective tend to deny psychological aspects, while those written by therapists sometimes tend to state that "it is always psychological." There are a few circumstances, however, in which some psychological causes are reasonably clear (four of which follow):

(1)Think back to a time that you lost weight and had at least partially achieved your weight loss goal. Did you then tend to be always on the go, too talkative, nervous, smoking/ drinking more or exercising too much? If so, it is likely that your extra pounds had some significant psychological basis.

(2)If you regained more than a pound a week of weight after a diet, at least one probable cause of your pre-diet extra weight was psychological (provided addictive allergies have been eliminated as a cause).

(3)Eating disorders such as bulimia and anorexia seem always to have some psychological basis.

(4)If your food binges are instigated by stress, psychological causes are most probable.

If your overweight problem started during your growing up years, then psychological problems were (and likely still are) important factors. If your extra pounds are at least partially caused by psychological traumas, these pounds may prove very difficult to lose. And I know of no treatment that can reliably offer a quick high rate of success. There are a few people who seem able to come to some quick psychological insights about their weight difficulties and readily translate these insights into permanent weight loss. These people are the lucky few. For most everyone else, the road to slimness is much longer and is often filled with detours and potholes. A svelte figure at the finish line is not guaranteed.*

There are several books available that describe psychological scenarios that cause overeating. Such books may or may not prove useful for you.

The most common scenario is that life events raise our stress levels and those of us who try to relieve stress by overeating then overeat. Maybe we don't want to face some emotions (like anger, rage, grief or love) or maybe we try to deny our competitiveness or aspects of our sexuality. Maybe we have significant childhood trauma associated with food: being overfed, being threatened with hunger, living with a food-manipulative parent, etc. Whatever emotions, or parts of ourselves or traumas we would like to avoid will cause us stress when circumstances trigger mind associations to such avoidances. Those with psychological food problems will then tend to eat to relieve the stress. Simple, yes. The ultimate solution is also simple - not to get stressed in such situations.

But this ultimate solution is much easier said than done. To change even one of our stress responses to a calm response usually takes energy, willingness and commitment to self-change.

It is often useful to consider fat as just a symptom, like a phobia, a headache or alcohol consumption. The psychological issues underlying all these symptoms are usually much the same. If you know your problems with fat are at least partially psychological, the next four chapters will be the chapters in this book likely to be most helpful to you.

LADY MACBETH'S DIET WAS DOOMED

You remember studying about her when you were in high school. She was the one who shouted something along the lines of "Out, damned fat! Out!" Her diet failed because of that statement. She emphasized what she did not want, the terrible looks of the fat, also her repulsion and revulsion. She displayed the worst type of self-talk. Self-talk like hers about a problem digs deeper ruts and causes added unhappiness, whether the problem is damned fat or a damned spot.

Instead, it is vital that you envision the positive goal or result. A mental image of a slimmer you will help you achieve the goal of slimness. Post a picture of yourself when you were much lighter. As you go by it several times during the day, *pretend* you are at that weight for a few seconds. If you have never been significantly lower in fatness than you are now, go find a photo of yourself. Cut your head from this photo and paste it on some magazine photo so that a body of reasonable (not skinny) proportions is below your head. Similarly, post this composite photo and *pretend* this is you several times daily as you walk by it. Practicing a mental image of yourself at your goal weight several times a day is highly desirable. You can strengthen your imaging capabilities by practicing images from *Creative Imagery* (sample on page 18).

This pretending or image-practicing is a common ingredient of successful weight loss programs. Do not follow this pretending with negative self-talk (like Lady MacBeth's). If you do find yourself concentrating on the negative (rolls of flab, anger at self, what a lousy person I am, how weak I am, etc.) try to deliberately change your mental focus. Change it away from the negative to *pretending* you are the person in that composite photo. This process of pretending or image-practicing will often elicit your internal growth impulses. These impulses will help point you along your road. The road

One Vital
Ingredient in
Most Successful
Weight Loss
Programs Is the
Image in Your
Mind of a
Slimmer You.

immediately ahead for you may be reading about nutrition, joining a support group, trying the Add-A-Carrot diet, reducing negative self-talk, getting some therapy or whatever seems appropriate for you now. If you care about success, then follow only one (sometimes two are OK) of the above roads at a time. A grand program following many roads simultaneously will most likely fail.

Lady MacBeth doomed herself to failure. Without pretending or image-practicing (either works well) described earlier, your weight loss program is most likely also doomed.*

FOOD BINGES ARE NATURAL PHENOMENA

No, I am not referring just to bears gorging themselves in preparation for hibernation. I am talking about our human heritage as hunter-gatherers. Hunter-gatherers must be opportunistic, for the Elberta peaches are at their succulent best for only a few brief days. Then there may be a wait for either the Delicious apples or the next variety of peach. Herring runs don't last long. Our heritage was to eat whatever was currently available, for it would often disappear shortly. If a windfall materialized after a time of want, you can bet our ancestors all gorged themselves on the windfall. Because binges do seem a natural part of our heritage, perhaps the best goal is not to try to eliminate them entirely from our behavioral repertoire. Have we <u>ever</u> successfully eliminated a natural behavior?

While I personally have never had excessive weight difficulties (always within twenty pounds of what I consider my best weight), I have had a history of food binges. They began in early childhood growing up with about 50-60 fruit trees, also many varieties of berries and grapes. Frequently during the summer most of my diet was just the latest from the tree, vine or bush. I then ate sparingly of or skipped the meals provided by Mom.

Gorging on the latest seasonal fruit is not likely to cause much weight gain if other foods are minimized. But that may not be true for ice-cream or other high-calorie binges. There are ways, however, of minimizing problems caused by binging on ice cream, cake, chocolates, etc. Planning and limits are the keys.

I plan a particular binge every year. I happen to be someone who likes fruitcake, and I won't stop eating it while it is in the house. Therefore, I plan that my next few meals after its arrival will be nothing but fruitcake. My weight gain is about half a pound. It is the planning ahead to eliminate all other foods that makes the difference. If for several days I snacked on the fruitcake besides regular meals, the calorie overload could well add 2-3 pounds to my weight. Not surprising to most of you fruitcake haters, I suppose, is the fact that I don't seem to want fruitcake for another year.

You probably noted that I didn't set any limits on how fast the fruitcake could be consumed. Of course not! It is a food binge, not a test of willpower. The limit I set was to eliminate other foods. If chocolate sauce is your thing, eliminate the ice cream and eat the sauce by itself; or if frosting is the *piece de resistance,* then eliminate the cake part from your frosting binge. If cake plus frosting is <u>it</u> for you, then a food binge that eliminates one or the other will not be satisfying and will probably not work for you. Make <u>your</u> food binge cake plus frosting. Be alive to lower-calorie diet foods in your supermarket. Downing a whole chocolate cake or a dozen custard eclairs of the Weight Watchers' variety may be just as satisfying as consumption of the higher-calorie alternatives.

Psychological food binges (i.e., triggered by stress in your life) will stop when your reactions to life events are that of calmness instead of stress. However, this could require a long process of growth and therapy. Meanwhile, if you cannot seem to avoid weight-gaining food binges, I suggest that you try for yourself a binge with two limits: (1)eliminating non-binge foods and/or (2)adding "rabbit food" at or near the beginning of each binge session. (The last sentence may seem like a laughable fantasy. But it is *your* idea about your helplessness facing a food binge that causes it to seem laughable. You are not that helpless unless you believe you are.) These possibilities may not work for your binges. You will not know unless you try. (If you try unsuccessfully, criticizing yourself is not helpful, but making a new choice *is* helpful.) If you cannot seem to eliminate food binges, the above methods are worth trying.

Gratefulness Exercise. *This will be most effective if read aloud.* I am grateful for the food I eat, its taste, its texture, its variety and its temperature. I appreciate that I have food. I particularly appreciate the existence of the following foods:_____(Fill your own blanks). A reminder- people who often feel appreciative or grateful are happier than most.

"Helpful" suggestions to overweight people about their weight are almost always unhelpful.

---

* See Appendix A

** Possible additions to your I-WANT-LIST (see Appendix C):
        I want to change the following food preferences_____.
        I want to weigh _____pounds (reasonable goal weight).
        I want to replace fat with flavor.
        I want to aerobically exercise 3X a week.
        I want to try pretending I am a much slimmer me.

Our emotional responses are caused by our <u>thinking</u> about the situation, not by the situation itself.

Chapter 8

Thinking

LET ME HIT YOU WITH A SLEDGEHAMMER

I routinely initiate a conversation with my clients that goes as follows: "We often have wrong ideas about our emotional reactions. They seem automatic and we tend to think they are automatic. They are not, for they depend upon how we think about a given situation. For example, if I came at you right now with my hands overhead threatening to attack you with a sledgehammer, how would you respond?" Presume for a moment that the client reacts with fear, saying something along the lines of, "I would run out the door." We then discuss how the client immediately evaluated the situation as unsafe and responded accordingly.

Then we discuss other possibilities such as getting angry and choosing to fight, or crying in the corner thinking about all of life's unfairness. The client might just laugh at me because the client knows that even if I did have a sledgehammer, the situation set up by me was only for demonstration purposes. Each of these possibilities depends upon the thinking of the person. The angry response derives from thinking that I should not be doing that, also a likely evaluation that I am not too strong for the client to fight. The crying response typically is evoked when old feelings of hopelessness are triggered. Finally, the laughter might come from thinking about a larger idea than just "a sledgehammer is close."

With this sledgehammer fantasy I am trying to make sure the client understands that our emotional responses depend upon our thinking processes much more than we think they do. <u>Even in an immediate situation of a poised sledgehammer there is no such thing as an emotional response common to everyone</u>.

This reasoning leads to, "If I can change how I think, I can change my emotions."* Does this mean I can get rid of my discomforts, my anger, my angst, my depression, my sadness, etc. just by thinking differently? Therapists who concentrate on changing your thinking processes would say "Yes!". (Talk therapy treatments of choice these days for depression are "thinking-type" therapies, not the emotionally-based therapies that one might initially think would be most effective with depression. Changing the thinking processes that cause the depression usually is much quicker than attempting to change the emotional processes themselves.)

THE TYRANNY OF JUDGMENTS

The judgments that usually cause us the most difficulties and distress are those that (1)judge situations/ others as right or wrong, (2)judge situations/ others as good or bad, or (3)judge situations as possible or impossible.

Humans have been making unhappy judgments for centuries. Shakespeare's Hamlet (*Hamlet* 2.2.255-256) expressed the happier accepting belief, "There is nothing good or bad but thinking makes it so." If the happier alternative has been known for so long, why hasn't it been followed? The reason is that we have been thoroughly indoctrinated in right/ wrong and good/ bad thinking. It is a natural thinking stage for children to pass through, and for adults to question. Most of us incorporated many such messages in our childhoods. We fail to see their tyrannical nature if we retain them as adults. For right/ wrong and good/ bad judgments about situations and others cause most of us much unhappiness *every day*.*

Another reason for our judgments is our poor self-esteem. Most of us have areas of our lives (our thinking, our emotions, our relationships, our sexuality, our addictions, our hangups, etc.) which we judge as not being OK, areas in which we have poor self-esteem. We then often try to make ourselves feel better at another's expense by judging them inferior in some way, "Look at how good I am in comparison." The macho judgment that women are inferior has its roots in poor male self-esteem; vulnerabilty, humaneness and caring are covered with a facade of strength. Current male-bashing also has similar roots in poor female self-esteem.

I personally strive *never* to feel or think that another's behavior or action is ever wrong or bad. I can always find some reasoning process to validate and accept what at first glance may seem very wrong or bad. Usually I do this by reaffirming my belief that each of us is perfect (as described later in this chapter) or by reaffirming my belief in Earth School that requires us to learn in ways that we might not consciously want (as described further in Chapter 11).

I can *always* find a possible reason why such situations are as they should be, instead of judging them to be wrong or bad. By reaffirming my belief that whatever is in our lives is in our best interest (more on this in Chapter 11), I am able to drop the *shoulds*. You too have the capability for dropping your *shoulds* by truly accepting the following happier ways of thinking: (1)we are always perfect, (2)we all are students here on Earth School and (3)everything in our lives is in our own best interest. Where the word *should* is used, there is an unhappy judgment.

Make sure not to judge yourself as bad or wrong when you find yourself making a judgment. For you and your judgments are, of course, perfect for that moment. The key is to begin changing your path toward the goal of dropping that judgment the next time that identical situation arises. Move to Stage IV *making a new choice*, rather than remain stuck in Stage II *blaming of oneself*. (See Chapter 4 for more on stages.)

Some judgments are still sometimes necessary as to right/ wrong or good/ bad for *me*. They are useful (not tyrannical) in selecting appropriate action. For example, I won't do that now because I learned in the past that it felt wrong, or because that possibility feels wrong for me at the moment. Such judgments do not apply to others. Just because I found something didn't work for me today or yesterday doesn't mean that it won't be exactly what you need to do (or, for that matter, what may wind up being appropriate for me in the future).

There are usually objections to this along the lines of, "If I dropped my judgments, then I wouldn't act appropriately to right the wrong." Not at all. If you put your hand on a hot stove you will take action in response to the pain. Later you can try to find out why you have repeated that behavior four times in the past week and why someone or something keeps making burns "right" for you. You respond to pain and discomfort perfectly, of course, for you now. Similarly, you do not need judgments to take appropriate action in response to situations that are not as you would like.

THAT IS THE WAY I AM

This phrase is widespread and is used to justify all sorts of behavior and ideas. And it probably is true today, but there is usually no thinking room

Nothing is miserable but what is thought so, and contrarywise, every estate is happy if he that bears it be content.

Boethius c. 500 A.D.

available to those who say it. Just because I am presently one way does not imply that I will be or have to be that way this afternoon. Unfortunately, the possibility of change is usually not even considered by those voicing the phrase, "That is the way I am" and its close relative, "That's the way we've always done it." The most important question that needs to follow that phrase is, "Do I want to continue to be that way?" Do I want to continue to be stuck with that unhappiness, that addiction, that low self-esteem, that depression, that loneliness, etc.? All too frequently we deny the possibility for change. Because we attempt no changes, stuckness becomes a self-fulfilling prophecy.

The possibilities for change are much greater than we typically envision. If your spiritual/ religious systems of beliefs cause you distress, then consider changing them! If you respond emotionally in unhappy ways, then you can always change your emotional responses if you are willing to really look at yourself. (Remember the sledgehammer earlier in this chapter?)

Consider adopting the following ultimate belief in self-responsibility: *if I am unhappy, then I need to change myself.** There are things which are usually not possible to change (i.e., some physical characteristics, one's sexual orientation and one's general personality characteristics). On the other hand, it is always possible to change one's actions and one's emotions.

If you hear the phrase, "That is the way I am," be on the lookout for frozen thinking and stuckness. Such rigidity is often evidence of Stage I *denial of problem* or Stage II *blaming others for the way I am.*

YOU MAKE ME UNHAPPY

This is the favorite accusation of millions. How convenient! I don't have to assume any responsibility for changing my unhappiness, and I can blame you for all of it. An unpleasant fact I usually overlook is that change by you is most unlikely to happen upon my demand. Therefore, I am likely to live forever with this unhappiness. "And it is all your fault that I am so stuck." Such is a common thought process of victims, and of those who are blaming ethnic groups for their problems.

It is only recently that major segments of the women's movement and the African-American movement have challenged the notion of being perpetual victims. These people are now choosing to take more responsibility for their own happiness and for their own lives, instead of remaining stuck in the blame game.

There is a major difference between the responses of children and the responses of adults. As children, many of us were squelched in any number of ways. Back then we <u>really were made unhappy</u> by what happened to us, (though most of us learned to cover over our unhappiness and to put on a compliant happy face). As children we usually had no real choice but to comply. If we believe this to be true today about our adult responses, then we are still letting others control our happiness, still acting the part of the helpless child. We have given our personal power away to others, most often to our most disliked others: white males, feminists, racists, sexists, homophobes and funda- mentalists.

The major question is then, what about "real" victims, like you and me and the groups to which we belong? Our choice to see ourselves as victims violates a number of religious and spiritual beliefs (like "God's Will," the "inky finger of fate" and "karma"). If we deeply hold such spiritual beliefs, is it possible for any of us ever to be victims? *No!* While such spiritual beliefs are held by a majority of the world's population, they still represent only a minority in the USA, albeit a fast-growing group that is nearing majority status. There is a choice to be made, believe in victimhood or believe in self-responsibility. The former guarantees unhappiness, whereas the latter permits a route out of unhappiness. Straddling these two beliefs is the most common USA choice today, believing in responsibility for some things but in victimization in other instances. Unfortunately, straddling does not lead to happiness, though it presently seems to be the socially-correct view for millions of us.

Do you want to continue <u>your</u> straddling?

YOU HURT MY FEELINGS-
THEREFORE YOU SHOULD CHANGE

Such is the trap into which millions of us fall, blaming others for our hurt feelings and making demands upon them for change. This is very similar to the preceding "You make me unhappy" trap which only leads to giving away of personal power, a continued lack of self-esteem and more power in the hands of those who so "hurt your feelings".*   To choose not to make one's happiness dependent upon others leads to real empowerment. And it is possible! But the possibility must first be recognized, secondly accepted as something desirable and thirdly actively pursued. The goal is to change from being hurt to being OK with whatever situation causes my hurts so that I am not hurt the next time that situation occurs. Do you want to be so empowered? Examination of similar childhood hurts will probably be the key to not being hurt next time.

STICKS AND STONES

On the playgrounds of our youth we all heard the old phrase, "Sticks and stones may break my bones but words will never hurt me." Unfortunately, many societal groups seem intent today upon claiming that words too always hurt. Whoever believes this gets to feel hurt a lot and is always at the whim of some person out there. Personal power is lacking.

It has only been in recent years that significant questioning of a hurt response to such verbal slings and arrows has developed. In the gay/lesbian movement there has been much recent discussion over the words "fag" and "queer" with many of the younger generation of gays and lesbians claiming those labels publicly. (Young blacks sometimes calling each other "nigger" has been a parallel development). By so doing, these younger men and women are increasing their self-esteem as well as making it impossible for homophobic/ racist bashers to bother them with words. This healthier response is an example of empowerment. A few happier activists are even coming to a belief that there is no such thing as adult verbal harassment. They are viewing claims of verbal victimization very differently. Their view is that claimants of verbal harassment have often thrown away possibilities for verbal repartee and capabilities for moving away.

The process of name-calling is typically based upon feeling not OK, and name-callers are trying to make themselves feel more powerful by using the process. If I call you a name and get you upset, then I temporarily feel more powerful because I had a powerful effect upon you. My self-esteem rises at your expense. I *project* my unhappiness on to you and *you take it on* if you allow yourself to be upset. If you do not get upset at my attempt, then I cannot dump my original unhappiness on you. Then I am left not only with my failure to successfully dump it on you but also with my original unhappiness to boot. Thus, if you're successful at being unbothered by my words, then I wind up more unhappy; and I'll probably quickly stop those words. This is a key element to understand, that name-callers will usually feel worse if you do not react to

*He with whom neither slander
that gradually soaks into the
mind, nor statements that
startle like a wound in the
flesh, are successful may
be called intelligent indeed.*

Confucius c. 500 B.C.

their name-calling. They will therefore be much quicker to stop such behavior than if you get visibly upset.

Someone call you a name? Whenever you hear such a name directed your way, thoughts along the lines of, "The name-caller is feeling weak right now" will help to prevent a possible hurt for you. Another useful self-thought is, "Whatever people say about me says nothing about me but a lot about them." We would be happier, feel more self-esteem and change the world dramatically if we all thought the following, "If I get upset by someone calling me a name, then I have given away my power and I need to make a different choice."

WE DIG THINKING RUTS

Three natural thinking patterns predominate in this culture. While as individuals we can change these patterns, we tend to have a favorite pattern that becomes automatic in many circumstances. Each of these patterns has pluses and minuses. Awareness of your favorite pattern can lead to lessening of the minuses associated with it.

Let me call the first, the *young* thinking pattern. This pattern is characterized by a strong sense of right and wrong. The right/ wrong thinking of this pattern was usually taken on, without any modification, directly from parenting figures, society, or religious teachings. There have been few, if any, changes in this thinking caused by direct experience since the pattern was incorporated, typically in childhood. Whoever exhibits this pattern has a sense of rightness about their actions, their thinking, their responses and their lives. Good self-esteem is possible. A definite plus! The minuses, however, can be excruciating if a person does not fit the right/ wrong image that has been incorporated. For example, some of my clients with this pattern have difficulty feeling childhood anger at parents because they "should honor their parents." They wind up displacing such "wrong" feelings onto others or covering them with addictions. To move beyond the minuses of this thinking pattern, there are two possibilities: (1)change the pattern or (2)change what is defined as "right." For those more comfortable with the next two patterns, just the awareness of being in this right/ wrong rut is often enough to start moving out of the pattern. For those most comfortable with right/ wrong, however, the necessity for changing what is thought of as "right" is likely to be essential.

A second thinking pattern commonly encountered in this culture is one resulting from the belief that you and I are really the same. If I think along these lines, you too (if only you weren't so defensive) must think the way I do. I'll call this *mature* thinking, using the terminology (*young, mature, old*) as described in *Messages from Michael* (Yarbro 1983, 132-150). But I intend no judgment about the relative value of these three thinking patterns. Togetherness and joining become important values for *mature* thinkers. Relationships are often rich and filled with empathy and understanding. Yes, a strong plus! Another plus for such *mature* thinkers is their willingness to find out what is right and wrong for themselves instead of just acquiring another's ideas without testing. The minuses often associated with this thinking pattern are enmeshments in unsatisfactory relationships, also anger, bewilderment and lack of understanding when people are really different. For example, if a *mature* thinking person with lots of idealism meets someone steeped in cynicism, understanding of the cynic will probably prove to be elusive. As there were for stuck *young* thinkers, there are two possibilities for stuck *mature* thinkers. One possibility is that the *mature* thinker can come to believe that in some ways we are very different, which is part of the *old* thinking pattern. Another possibility is to judge others as underdeveloped because they don't think the way the *mature* thinker does. Such judgments create the exact opposite of what the *mature* thinker wants (togetherness, unity, and relationship).

The *old* thinking pattern is, "You do your thing and I'll do mine." There is no need for us to be the same. Differences are celebrated, provided they don't interfere with my path. This pattern's minuses of less togetherness and less certainty about many issues, while difficult, need not necessarily cause distress. This can be a thinking pattern of inner contentment and is recommended whenever possible.

SIZE AND CONTENTS OF THE UNCONSCIOUS

If I asked people to consider the size of their unconscious minds and demanded they select from (pea-sized / melon-sized / Montana-sized), most would pick pea-sized or melon-sized. Historically, the unconscious was considered just a small part of us with a few repressed memories and traumas, perhaps pea-sized. In recent years, with the increased study of dreams, images, consciousness and more acceptance of such things as ESP (about half our population now believes in ESP), the role of the unconscious is now often believed to at least rival that of the conscious mind. While there is no so-called scientific proof for my belief, it seems clear to me that my unconsious is so much more powerful and knowing than my conscious mind that I would pick Montana-sized. If your unconscious is as big as Montana, then think of its vast potential! This allows for the possibility that your entire self (including whatever one might consider as a Higher Power a la 12-Step Programs) is *completely* in charge of your life. Your Montana-sized unconscious would obviously intermingle with others' Montana-sized selves. Such mingling of unconscious fields has obvious similarities to the collective-unconscious idea that was postulated by one of psychology's pioneers, Carl Jung.

More important than your thoughts about the size of your unconscious are your thoughts about its contents. Historically, it has been popular to believe in a dark, evil, dangerous unconscious that needed strict controls to avoid disaster. What a damaging belief to have about the unconscious mind! It is not a happy life being unable to trust the unknown parts of oneself and having to distrust impulses and dreams (the fountainheads of much that is grand and wonderful about us).* Yes, there may be some traumatic memories contained in the unconscious, but to my thinking they are a small price to pay for creativity, play, joy, spontaneity, spirituality, self-trust and happiness.

I suggest that you trust and explore all impulses. I do not recommend <u>acting</u> upon all. But they are <u>always</u> important to examine and to trust as valid on some level. If the likely consequences of following an impulse are acceptable, then <u>acting</u> on the impulse is also recommended.

So how to respond to an unacceptable impulse, say to harm someone? I repeat: the impulse has valid information for you, the action is not appropriate. You probably do hate that person. Can you change that hatred without denying it? Do you need to pretend that person is in front of you and express your hatred to them in fantasy? Should the hatred be directed at someone else (see Chapter 9)? It is important to examine unacceptable impulses with the question, "What do I need to learn from this?". If the impulse still comes back, you haven't learned your lessons yet. Therefore, make a new Stage IV *choice.*

We have all received training in distrusting our impulses. Such training keeps us stuck in many areas of our lives.

NATURE VS. NURTURE VS. LIFEPLAN

We have all heard the debate about which aspects of our beings are caused by genes and which are caused by upbringing. What one never hears in this debate is the possibility that there might be a third alternative, what I am referring to is a lifeplan. Could it be that we come into our lives with some definite unconscious plan to learn certain things, to be associated in particular ways with certain people, to have specific attributes and to do good (or not so good) works? A lifeplan of one description or another is part of the belief systems of much of the world, but we here in the USA have in recent history tried to find almost all the answers under the microscope or in the laboratory. Our belief has typically been that all the answers will be found there; other possibilities have been often scorned.

The evidence for such a thing as a lifeplan is all around us if we but look. Look at little children and how incredibly different they are personally and psychologically from one another. They are vastly different from their parents and grandparents even in the earliest weeks and months of their lives. Look at the "amazing" synchronous events which often occur to allow many of us to find exactly the right job, the right mate or the best path. Instead of trying to prove the roots of homosexuality to be nature or nurture, might the truth be elsewhere in an unconscious lifeplan? How come there are always many who avoid contracting the current plague despite much exposure to the disease? The plague in the Middle Ages is one example. The current AIDS plague is another example; some whom one would surely expect to contract the disease just don't catch it. Scientists might claim "unknown genes". But a specific unconscious lifeplan that needed to avoid the disease seems a more likely possibility to me, a possibility usually completely out of the realm of thinking of such scientists.

THE PERFECTION THAT YOU ARE NOW

A most liberating and happiness-generating belief that one can have is to believe in the perfection of everyone around. Not only is Mother Teresa perfect, but so is Saddam Hussein and everyone in between. "Sure, sure, another bit of semantics or idealistic intellectualism," I hear you respond. Not at all.

My unhappy thinking patterns, my unhappy emotional responses, my couch-potato body, my lousy relationships and all the rest of my symptoms are perfect. I gained each and every one of them precisely (usually unconsciously) in response to events in my past. For example, if I was traumatized to give up my anger, grief, love and sexuality, then I needed to give them up to get the maximum acceptance (or minimum punishment) in my childhood. If I still don't have them, (anger, grief et al), then so far it has not been safe for me to regain them. I continue to need my defenses against such dangerous (to my neurotic/ skewed self) feelings. Therefore, each symptom is still perfect and needed. Genuine belief in this perfection can lead to *real* acceptance of oneself and others. (It is also the essence of real forgiveness discussed earlier in Chapter 4.)

I can then hear you say, "But if I accept that symptom, I won't want to change it or I won't be energetic in my efforts to change it." Not true. What will happen is that by truly accepting its perfection, then you will stop the self-recriminations, the low self-esteem and the negative judgments, none of which do anything but impede your progress toward making the changes that might eliminate the symptom. You may often wind up worrying about the future or ruminating about the past if you do not *accept* the perfection that is you and me and everyone else. By accepting a symptom as perfect and still wanting it to be different, then the next step for you usually becomes obvious.

"But I still want my symptom to be gone and when I don't get what I want I get unhappy," I hear you respond. Please read the next section.

BE HAPPY GETTING WHAT YOU DON'T WANT

This seems impossible to achieve, to be happy when we get things we don't want. The reason it seems impossible is that we *believe* we should be unhappy when we don't get what we want. (In all of this, there is the following truth: if we believe such a situation calls for unhappiness, we <u>will</u> be unhappy.) The essence of changing such unhappiness is to change the underlying belief that it is normal and natural to become unhappy when we don't get what we want.

If this guy would <u>change</u> his thinking, he would be much happier.

Having to change one's ice cream flavor if they have run out of chocolate is not a situation in which most of us would agree that unhappiness would be automatic. There would be far less agreement about other "more important" wants such as a desired new job or love interest that failed to develop. Yet it really is in how we think about these denied wants. If I start emphasizing in my head all the reasons why that new desired job was *not* ideal or emphasizing my spiritually-based belief that "my higher self (or God/ Higher Power/ karma) makes sure I always get what I really need," then unhappiness is not likely. (And if it does appear, then I have self-therapy to do.)

Recently during the Mississippi River flooding, several big-city reporters were astonished at the reactions of a few of the midwesterners who had lost homes and livelihoods to the river. For some of those experiencing such catastrophic losses were not unhappy or stressed out. (Such losses are expected as a part of living close to the land or sea by farmers and fishermen. Therefore, unhappiness during such natural disasters might be for a very limited time, perhaps just for a few minutes.) Those incredulous reporters didn't realize that they were the ones who probably could have used therapy most at that moment!

There may be childhood successes as well as childhood trauma associated with this belief in automatic unhappiness when I don't get what I want. Many of us as toddlers learned to threaten a tantrum or tears in the supermarket when denied a favorite food item; this often resulted in our gaining the item. Thus, we learned that we sometimes could get what we wanted by being unhappy. Therefore, we sometimes continue the process today by hoping or demanding that others respond to our unhappiness or hurt feelings or depression. Those who did have such early successes in getting others to respond to threatened unhappiness will have difficulty giving up this mode of personal relating.

As traumatized children, on the other hand, we were not successful in getting what we actually needed, items such as enough real love and acceptance. We wanted and needed these items and did not get them. Most of us learned that not getting what we *needed* did lead to unhappy feelings and trauma. Our childish minds then interpreted that experience as also meaning that not getting what we *wanted* was the cause of the unhappiness. Not true.

This unhappy belief (if I don't get what I want, I'll be unhappy) is widespread in this culture. If you wish to read further, I suggest Kaufman's *To Love Is To Be Happy With*. Just ridding this culture of this one belief would do worlds for our society's happiness. *I can be happy no matter whether I get what I want or not.** Changing yourself in this regard is not necessarily that difficult.

Often the most difficult part is just coming to realize that such a change *might* be possible.

YOU'LL SEE IT WHEN YOU BELIEVE IT

The statement, "You'll see it when you believe it," is contrary to much of what we have learned in this materialistic society. Materialism is not just the gathering of goods to me but also includes the belief that if I can't sense it with one or more of my five senses, then it is suspect. The idea that one might choose to believe something *before* actually sensing it is considered daft. Nevertheless, such a so-called daft idea can lead to much increased happiness and the possibility of manifesting the impossible. Impossible cures, improbable events, unexpected windfalls and happy surprises await those who believe (or pretend or imagine) first. For more detailed information I recommend an important book by Wayne Dyer and titled the same as the above subheading, *You'll See It When You Believe It.*

Is it the belief in abundance that triggers the windfall? Is it the belief in a cure for an incurable disease that triggers the healing? Is it the belief in oneself that triggers a creative leap? Is it the pretend-belief in thinness that triggers the reduction in weight for an overweight person? One common pattern seems to be that my unconscious often follows my conscious wishes and my conscious visualizations, thus producing so-called impossible cures and unexpected windfalls. Unfortunately for my conscious ego, my lifeplan may interfere with manifesting some of my conscious wishes. For example, if I am learning the lessons of relationship this lifetime, then a conscious wish on my part for years of isolation will not likely occur.

My judgments as to the possibility or impossibility of a future event can be as tyrannical as my other right/ wrong and good/ bad judgments discussed earlier in this chapter. If I judge that event to be impossible, then it likely will be impossible for me. Yet if I judged it as possible, it might be. If you believe that you can cure your incurable cancer (there are people who have gone before you who have done so), then it may be possible. Dr. Carl Simonton has discovered important truths about selfhealing by cancer patients by the selfuse of imagery. This healing has confounded conventional medical wisdom.

Could my beliefs in a dangerous and unjust world be causing added violence and injustice in my life? Do my cynicism and pessimism draw dreadful experiences to me, instead of being the result of such experiences?

"You will see it when you believe it" may initially seem a bit crazy, but if true, it implies that we would serve ourselves best by cultivating our optimism and our hopefulness. Pollyanna was obviously happy. Could it also be true that she was much more intelligent and wise than her detractors?

UNHAPPY THINKING QUIZ**

Try answering the following quiz rapidly.

    T F   I make a number of judgments about other peoples' behavior, particularly the behavior of _____.

    T F   Often I say "that is the way I am."

    T F   Others often make me unhappy.

    T F   I worry a lot.

    T F   I ruminate a lot about the past.

    T F   I often have hurt feelings because of others' inconsiderateness.

    T F   Nasty names naturally hurt people.

    T F   Impulses had best be squelched.

    T F   I am flawed at the moment.

    T F   When I don't get what I want, I get unhappy.

Quiz Answers. Each statement you answered *True* shows where your thinking is causing you unhappiness. Changing your thinking about *any* such statement will make for more inner contentment for you. If you answered *False* to all, then perhaps you are ready for sainthood! (Or you may be one who has much knowledge of thinking-based therapies such as Option, Rational-Emotive or Cognitive-Behavioral.)

YOU GET WHAT YOU BELIEVE IN

Can this be true? I get what I believe in? I know your immediate response may be, "No, that's not true". However, I ask you to hang in there with the possibility of that statement being the truth. For freedom lurks just over the horizon. If I can get over my beliefs in my own sickliness, obesity, and being persecuted, then these will, according to this theory, no longer be drawn into my life. "But the fat, sickness and persecution are all around! Open your eyes!"; I hear you respond. I suggest that you hold that unhappy response at arm's length and <u>practice</u> instead the happier beliefs for a time as in the next exercise.

Growth Exercise. Visualize (or pretend) several times a day for the next two weeks (1)being at your appropriate weight, (2)health and vitality, and/ or (3)love from <u>and towards</u> all your persecutors. (Pick only those visualizations appropriate to your difficulties.)

If you do this exercise, things will most likely start to change for you in very positive directions. Then you will have experienced some of the truth in the statement: *you get what you believe in.* Experience, my own and that of others, suggests that it may take months or years before you fully believe the statement. *You get what you believe in* has unhappy ramifications with respect to how undesirable unhappy beliefs really are (they attract more unhappiness and draw unhappy people/ situations into one's life). For more, perhaps you wish to read chapter 11, where the information closely parallels this section.

HOW CLOSE CAN WE COME TO "HAPPILY EVER AFTER"?

This culture makes a huge investment in the happily-ever-after belief. Not only do most of the tales we tell our children end this way, but we have a number of similar beliefs that keep tripping us up as adults.

A common unhappiness-causing adult belief in "happily ever after" is, "If I do the right things, then I should be rewarded with happiness." Anger and outrage often follow when the result seems to be more like punishment than a reward. Justice is supposed to prevail, according to many of us, yet it all too frequently seems most blind and capricious. We do not have to give up our belief in justice, just our belief that justice will happen in our lifetime. Punishment by God or by karma outside this lifetime will suffice, thank you. We don't have to try to spend herculean amounts of time, energy and money to make it happen here on earth. More than anything else, it is our failure as a society to have satisfying spiritual beliefs that propels our overzealous concentration on our justice system. We spend billions suing each other, we spend billions on frivolous appeals and we personally await jury verdicts (years later) before we let our old wounds go.

You really can come close to "happily ever after," but the necessity for *some* unhappiness for a limited amount of time must be accepted. Our growth processes are commonly triggered by our feelings of unhappiness with a given event or person. It is often necessary to go *through* a certain amount of unhappy feelings before one feels happy. However, that process need not take long. We tend to accept days and weeks of mild depression as OK, but they are not necessary if we are willing to face the feelings behind the mild depression. We tend to expect many months of grief after a death, but often that can be shortened dramatically. As a rule, (this will vary from one person to the next and from this week to the next), try for 23 1/2 hours of happiness a day during normal times. Stay with your unhappiness only for a short time, but do not attempt to avoid it entirely. Unhappiness can be postponed for a few hours or even a few days, but its complete avoidance will likely increase the severity and duration of every one of your symptoms.

There are several "thinking" therapies available and I have made reference to them in the footnote below. "Thinking" therapies are often the most productive in terms of happiness for your therapy dollar. You can also make worthwhile thinking changes by using this book or by reading others.

---

* See Appendix A

** Possible additions to your I-WANT-LIST (see Appendix C):
   I want to change my thinking about _____ (see Unhappy Quiz earlier in this chapter).
   I want to read Kaufman's *To Love Is to be Happy With* and *Happiness Is a Choice.*
   I want to read about Option, Rational-Emotive or Cognitive-Behavioral therapy
      approaches.

*A Time to Weep
and a Time to Laugh;
a Time to Mourn,
and a Time to Dance....
a Time to Love
and a Time to Hate...*

Ecclesiastes 3:3, 3:8

Chapter 9
Emotional Health = Mental Health

EMOTIONAL HEALTH

What is emotional health anyway? A useful definition of emotional health is the ability to express all emotions appropriately. Those who have this ability are surely mentally healthy. Being emotionally stuck is often the best indicator of current lack of emotional health. I might be stuck in depression or stress, stuck in anger at my favorite targets, stuck in obsessive fears, or stuck in perpetual guilt or shame. Obviously, this indicator of emotional health suggests that many of us lack emotional health much of the time.*

An outstanding example of emotional health is the average two-year-old, who often displays a full range of emotions. Emotions are usually freely expressed and felt by the two-year-old, and therefore stuckness in any one emotion for more than a couple of minutes doesn't happen often. Once felt, emotions change. Without emotional change one stays discomfited, clear evidence of skewed emotional expression. This is a commonly overlooked truism about emotions - once they are felt properly, they disappear, thus making room for the next feeling or emotion. (The root of the word, e-motion, implies motion or change.)

ANGER AND OUTRAGE

It has become politically-correct these days to be outraged by this, that, or the other. *Of course* as a fundamentalist I am outraged by gays. *Of course* as a gay I am outraged by fundamentalists. *Of course* as a woman I am outraged by the white male patriarchy. *Of course* as an African-American I am outraged by

91

racism. *Of course* I am outraged by the right-to-life movement/ abortion rights. *Of course* as a male I am outraged by some feminists. My question for those so outraged is, "Do you like the feeling of outrage?". "Of course not," might be a typical response. Then why not explore the possibility of changing your response? "That's outrageous!", I hear you respond, outraged at a new target, this author. For the moment, I ask that you please just accept that outrage is an *unhappy* feeling.

Outrage at particular people or groups <u>always</u> stems from a thought pattern of "they should not be ....". (And in almost all cases those "villainous" people or groups being judged think they are doing the right thing!) Outrage is a judging pattern that fails to <u>accept</u> reality as it is. In truth, those outrageous folks are that way. They just do not live up to my expectations.

> **<u>Anger Tip.</u>** There are few "always" in therapy. Here is one of them: anger (including irritation, rage, hatred, etc.) is *always* based upon unfulfilled expectations.* If I can let go of my expectations, I will not feel angry.

If I keep my expectations, I keep my outrage and my unhappiness. I may fail to see the reasons for those who outrage me to be the way they are, and instead of accepting their differences, I cling to my outrage. Why?

Often part of the reasoning process in "why we should keep our outrage" is the belief that we won't take any action to change those outrageous people unless we feel anger. Why do we believe that? Do we need anger to propel ourselves to get an ice cream cone or to go after our true lo ves? Of course not! Not only is our outrage an unhappy experience for us, but it is also the <u>least</u> effective way to elicit change in those at whom the outrage is directed. If someone is raging at us, our priority is to defend, not to listen. Often we keep our outrage because it allows us to project the entire problem "out there" and to consider ourselves flawless and blameless. Acknowledging that our outrage reflects unwillingness to accept reality might force self-examination of our individual and collective psychological reasons for being outraged, thus moving us beyond the unhappiness of Stage II outrage.

I often cling to my outrage for psychological reasons. Most likely I use such current-day outrage as a compensation for the fact that I am unwilling to face my childhood outrage. Instead of facing the childhood anger and hatred locked within me, I express it indirectly by splaying it over my favorite targets of today. Or if I have faced most of those angry feelings of childhood, then my outrage may be compensation for my unwillingness to feel my childhood pain, grief and hopelessness (more on these difficult feelings in Chapter 10). Outrage at others is a favorite projection. Instead of seeing the problem as belonging to me, I see it as "out there".

Am I saying that you should never feel outrage? No, but I am saying that there is always a happier response. If you do feel outrage, it is correct for you as your current emotional response. The tough choices are (1)whether you want that response in the future and (2)whether you are willing to do some work to change your response. You first must decide if you want to change.

My Problem Is That My Anger Keeps Coming Back. This is a clear indicator that the issue has not been resolved. Your anger is skewed. It is either off target, and/or the wrong emotion is being expressed. Yes, this does imply that I consider much of the socially-correct bashing so common these days to be skewed, neurotic or off-target (you pick the adjective).

It has been my experience that my clients' anger difficulties most often have their roots in childhood trauma knots that my clients do not wish to face. The part of those trauma knots that is most often avoided is *hatred*, childhood hatred. Until those clients are willing to feel that hatred, they continue to have difficulties with anger. Facing that aspect of trauma is discussed in the next chapter of this book.

Emotionally Healthy Adults (with respect to anger)

1. are comfortable with anger and hatred, their own and others.

2. do get angry or fearful when physically threatened (fight/flight).

3. generally do not get angry when verbally attacked.

4. are able to change their responses. This implies that the next time
an identical angry-making circumstance occurs (except #2 above), they
do not get angry.

5. get angry rarely. Once they express the anger, it does not return.

6. do not dredge up old arguments because that old anger is long gone.
They are genuinely able to forgive.

Obviously, few of us achieve the above. Nevertheless, you will be much happier the closer you are able to duplicate the above anger responses of emotionally

Is This You?

Do you want to change yourself so
that the next time
identical circumstances arise you
feel a happier emotion?

healthy adults. Do you want to make it your personal long term goal to change some of your anger responses?

LOVE

The Eskimos have perhaps 60 words in their language for the word *snow*. They would no doubt feel very cramped with just our one word, for it would fail to adequately describe the various manifestations of snow so important to them. Our language similarly tries to cram many meanings into the word *love*.

Love (infatuation): this is the stuff of "falling in love," living in a rosy magical glow, etc. My beloved has no faults and is perfect in almost every respect. We shall live happily ever after. This is typically a state of <u>denial</u>, overlooking many things all too obvious to many of those around me. This type of love does not last, though many wish it would. Many keep pursuing this type of love for years without realizing that it must fail because it is <u>not</u> reality.

Love (which lasts): this is the stuff of actively caring for another and accepting the other as they are. This type of love is a <u>decision</u>.* One decides to accept the other totally, without reservation, and with eyes open. The other's faults are both seen and accepted. The true practitioner of this type of love can honestly give their loved ones the *Love Story* message, "Love means not ever having to say you're sorry" (Segal 1970, 131). For whatever so-called harm was done, the loved one is accepted and known to be OK. Many of us achieve this type of love only with pets or small children. Active involvement, while not essential to feeling love, is essential to an ongoing relationship; and its absence will typically be felt as a lack of love. In this culture many of us experienced the physically and/or emotionally absent father, who may have felt love for us, but from whom we often did not *receive* the feeling of love.

Love (the bastardized version most of us give and receive): this is conditional love. I'll love you if you do this, or act that way, or perform in some way that meets my expectations. Most of us received conditional love as children. Most of us needed then to hide our hating, our sexuality, our tears and/or our vulnerabilities because those human qualities were not accepted by parents or society. So we put on a performance by denying those unapproved aspects of ourselves to get the maximum number of strokes. It was not real acceptance of ourselves we received as children, just an absence of condemnation of the aspects we hid. Conditional love is widespread today among adults in most relationships. We couldn't possibly love them if they do this, or they dislike us, or they have the wrong views, etc. If you don't act the way I think you *should* act, then I'll reject you. You are totally unacceptable to me if you lie, cheat, two-time me, hate me, treat my family wrong, don't agree with me on issues, etc. But if you do jump through my required hoops, then I'll love you (conditionally, obviously). Conditional love created many trauma knots in us as children which we then later as adults need to untie.

Love (the feeling): there are some of us who cannot feel the feeling of love for others. It was trained out of us by the traumas of childhood. For those of us so suffering, (often unknowingly), more men than women, there will be avoidances of (1)close relationships and (2)the words "I love you". If this is your difficulty, then the most important step you can take is to *decide you want to feel love*. To actually feel loving toward others will probably take some time and perhaps therapy. There are even more of us who do not "get" the feeling of love when it is directed toward us. We slough it off without actually receiving it. A decision is also required here as a first step, the decision to want to be able to receive love.

Love (its verbal expression): the words *I love you*. Many of us have difficulties with those three little words. Those who have been "toughened" in their childhoods or by life will often be unable to say, "I love you." Some of us will place a huge barrier between ourselves and those words, a barrier such as: "I can't say them until I <u>know</u> the other person is my life-mate." Thus we fail to acknowledge that *we* have a problem. The difficulty with saying the words *I love you* without any feeling attached (i.e., caring seems to be missing) is also prevalent, and is particularly confusing to children. For example, children <u>know</u> their silent or angry alcoholic dads don't care much. But their effusive moms, with their thousands of supposedly caring words, can cause a lifetime of confusion. The ability to say the words *I love you* <u>with feeling</u> is essential. The ability to appropriately express those words in a nonsexual context to men, women and children is a good indicator of emotional health.

Love (its physical expression): hugs. To be able to lovingly hug men, women and children is a part of the repertoire of healthy adults. Unfortunately, many have learned to equate hugs with sex. This leads to homophobic avoidance of same-sex hugs, particularly among men. Often one healthy first step for men is to allow the thought into their minds that such hugs are no more sexual than those given children. (Chapter 5 has more on touching/ hugging.)

Love (its sexual expression): lust. Sexual behavior is usually accompanied by a feeling of significant lust, which may or may not occur within the context of a significant relationship with that sexual partner. The feeling of love (described in an earlier paragraph) may or may not accompany the lust/ sexual behavior. Many of us, because of training and/or trauma, have lost either our lust or our ability to have sexual relations with others. Either loss is much to our detriment (more on such sexual difficulties in Chapter 15).

Emotionally Healthy Adults (with respect to love)

1. are comfortable saying the words *I love you* to men, women and children in a feeling way.

2. are comfortable hugging men, women and children in a feeling way.

3. "get" (actually physically receive) the feeling of love when it is directed their way.

4. express their total lovingness (emotionally, physically, verbally and lustily) with a particular partner.

5. decide to love another and then do so.

Few of us achieve all the above. Nevertheless, you will be much happier the closer you duplicate the above responses concerning love. Therefore, do you want to make it your personal long term goal to make some changes in how you feel, express and think about love? (I hope you do.)

SADNESS

Who wants such an unpopular feeling? YOU DO, if you want to be happy. This may seem bizarre, but it most assuredly is true. For unless you are able to feel sadness (and its relatives: sobbing, grief and tears), you will forever be avoiding sadness. Avoidance makes you prone to addictive behavior, psychosomatic symptoms, high levels of anxiety and acting-out skewed behavior. Sadness is a natural feeling which, if unfelt, just stays in our array of unresolved trauma knots. As with other emotions, feel it and it will go away. Resist feeling it and it hangs around forever, periodically erupting inappropriately in our body's attempt to rid itself of associated trauma knots.

It has been most unfashionable to cry, most particularly in the 1950s and 1960s. Negative judgments were commonly made about those who did so in public. Politicians for many years avoided anything even remotely connected to tears. Today that seems to be changing. We all need to feel sadness and grief at times. If we are not to remain emotionally disabled, then we need to allow whatever sobs need to wrack us and whatever tears need to roll down our cheeks.

Common inhibiting beliefs are: (1)my tears would never stop, (2)tears or sobbing would show weakness (unmanliness too), (3)others would disapprove.

(1)Of course your tears would stop. Don't histrionic tears of even the most melodramatic person eventually stop? The real fear typically is that of loss of control. If I let the tears or sobbing start, then I won't be able to stop them. They <u>will</u> stop of their own accord, probably sooner than later. You <u>will</u> stop them if you need to do so in an emergency or if that is your choice.

(2)Do tears and sobbing show weakness? NO, THEY SHOW STRENGTH!* That is, of course, a different view from what many of us learned as children. Nevertheless, it takes strength and courage to allow all one's emotions (particularly ones that might be criticized) to be expressed. To be authentic emotionally shows much more strength of character than to hide one's unpopular parts. The person who cannot or will not express the natural human expressions of tears and sobbing could be considered emotionally crippled.

(3)There are still some who disapprove of almost any expression of sadness, because they are afraid to feel it themselves. The phrase "break down into tears" captures the essence of this disapproval. I have hopes the media will soon come to realize that use of "break down" in that context is unhelpful to society and fosters continuation of macho-male stereotypes. In the 1990s, given many tears by famous males, disapproval of sadness and tears is definitely on the wane. Hallelujah!

One common dilemma facing us in our relationships is what to do when our partner starts crying. Do we attempt to comfort or do we maintain a respectful distance? This may be likened to serving another person fried eggs. You probably wouldn't serve someone a fried egg unless you asked beforehand whether they liked it sunny-side-up or turned-over. Likewise, we had best check with our particular partners beforehand to find out their likes and dislikes concerning comfort vs. distance when they cry. Then one gives that partner what they want. (Be alive to the fact that such wants may change over time, perhaps even from one time to the next. Both partners need to keep communicating.)

Emotionally Healthy Adults (with respect to sadness)

1. are comfortable with sadness, their own and others.

2. allow their own wracking sobs and tears.

3. feel good once their sobs and tears have been expressed.

4. are not stuck in recurring sadness, which happens when (a)hatred is blocked, (b)one's spiritual system is an unhappy one or if (c)childhood hopelessness is being blocked.

The closer we get to the above, the happier we will be. Do you want to change some of your ideas and behavior concerning sadness? If yes, then make your desired change(s) a goal.

FEAR

Fear plays an essential role in nearly all our psychological problems. Whenever trauma knots get triggered by our thoughts or by life events, fear arises. For it was fear of fully experiencing the original traumas that caused them originally to be tied in knots. Stress is fear.*

Fear shows itself in a multiplicity of ways. Those who were not loved will often sabotage their close relationships because of fear of being loved. Those who couldn't ask their parents for love will fear doing so with their current partners. Those who were trained to be tough will be afraid of signs of weakness (weakness according to their definition). Those who learned to be afraid of anger will often have fearful rationales for their avoidance of anger. Phobias, anxieties and depression are symptoms that often have significant roots in fear. Whatever trauma knots you have not resolved will cause you fear (i.e., stress).

Often we deny the fear, switching instantaneously to anger, addiction, depression, or other favorite dodges. It is often an important first step just to recognize the fear as fear. The process of change can then start, for one can examine the situation more rationally to see if fear is warranted. Perhaps something different next time can be experienced instead of getting locked in

Skewed emotions are like the horse shown above, headed the wrong way. They lead us nowhere. They give us the illusion of usefulness because they temporarily help us feel better.

the fear. Much fear is fear acquired as a child, which frequently may be discarded once it is in full conscious awareness. If it cannot be discarded, then examining the relevant trauma knots may be required.

There are many available self-help books with the word *fear* in their titles. They can be most valuable, for almost all therapy problems have some roots in fear. Some of these books suggest turning fear into love. Some suggest facing the fear. Another prescription is to act *counterphobically* (doing what one fears). When you are in your favorite bookstore, I suggest perusing the self-help aisle. If one of the available books appeals to you, it will probably be right for you.

Emotionally Healthy Adults (with respect to fear)

1. are not fearful or anxious for other than brief periods of time.

2. will experience fear (or anger) if physically threatened. (This is the natural fight/ flight response.)

3. are able to confront and change their fear-causing beliefs to happier beliefs. Thus, they do not get stuck in stress.

4. are often capable of appropriate action, despite high levels of fear.

Few of us achieve the above, yet wouldn't you be happier if you could? Perhaps one of the above possibilities could be a long term goal for you.

STUCK FEELINGS

There are several so-called emotions that are inherently stuck. Feel them and you stay in them. They remain around forever, unless the real truths beneath them are felt. Some inherently stuck feelings are: guilt, jealousy, depression, humiliation, shame and degradation. Feeling them for any longer than it is necessary to recognize them is not productive. Be on the lookout *behind* these stuck feelings for *other* unwanted feelings (such as childhood hurt, love, fear, rage or grief) which, if felt, could help change the immobility.

It is often but not always true that: (1)guilt indicates repressed anger at early parenting figures, (2)jealousy indicates a fear of loss of early parenting figures, (3)depression indicates repression of difficult feelings, and (4)humiliation, shame and degradation indicate difficulties with self-esteem (or with judging others if others are judged as humiliated, shamed or degraded). It is suggested that you use this paragraph as a likely starting point for exploration of your own stuck emotions.**

FEELING BAD

Feeling Bad? Make a new choice! The prescription is very simple and valid too. But finding the right choice or a happy choice may be difficult. We may have to choose and experience several unhappy alternatives (which might make us feel worse) before we find one that will be right for us. But if we persevere with our old unhappy ways, we are stuck, and we will emote in a skewed manner.

SKEWED EMOTIONAL EXPRESSION IS RAMPANT

We see skewed (i.e. twisted, neurotic, off-target, etc.) emotional expression everywhere and rarely label it as such. (By so labeling it, this may prove to be a most unpopular paragraph.) Hurt feelings that keep on happening over and over can be labeled skewed, neurotic or off-base. Guilt, shame or jealousy that keeps persisting is evidence that e-motions are blocked and unwilling to be faced. For adults, nearly all adult anger in the present at politicians, spouses, children, neighbors and favorite targets is skewed. Tears that don't stop imply skewness. Why so much skewed emotional expression? The reason is that 97% of us learned in our growing-up years to stuff one or more of our emotions (causing trauma knots as described in Chapter 3). Stuffed emotions are remembered by our bodies and our unconscious minds, and they act like internal irritants. They keep grating on us, keep causing us anxiety and keep leading us into addictive situations in which we can discharge the irritating energy in a skewed fashion. A skewed discharge reduces our anxiety, although temporarily. A discharge of most of the important emotions of the original trauma knot, on the other hand, usually eliminates the knot.

How can you tell what the truth is behind the skewness? There are some tendencies that are useful to know. If your anger or sadness is skewed, the most likely place to look for the truth is your own kid anger or kid sadness associated with your unexplored childhood traumas. If you perceive your guilt to be skewed, then childhood anger is the most likely culprit. Skewed expression of love most commonly starts in one's youth with skewed or absent parental expressions of love. These are all just likelihoods. We can and do use skewed love in the present to compensate for stuffed anger in our past. We use guilt and shame to compensate for stuffed love in our past. We can use almost any emotion as skewed compensation for another. Our feelings of relief in such circumstances, however, will be temporary.

The often lengthy process of discovering and experiencing your own emotional truths will provide permanent relief. (That does not imply you need be unhappy for much of that time or that the process necessarily will take up huge blocks of your time.) It does mean that there will be moments of difficulty, moments of stress, and moments of pain. If one learns to e-<u>mote</u> in a non-skewed way, however, then these will be <u>moments</u> of difficulty, instead of <u>continuous</u> difficulty**. If one keeps on stuffing the emotion(s), then the resultant stress <u>will</u> be ever present. To that I say, "No thanks!".

For maximum happiness, contentment and inner peace, we need all our emotions, not just the pleasant ones.

* See Appendix A
**Possible additions to your I-WANT-LIST (See Appendix C):
   I want to be able to fully express my emotions.
   I want to avoid stuck emotions.
   Whenever I feel bad, I want to look for a new choice.

*Please note the crowds
clamoring to enter
the above Therapy 4-H Club.*

Chapter 10

Therapy 4-H Club

PEOPLE ARE NOT FLOCKING
TO JOIN THIS CLUB

People do avoid the first three H's of this mythical Therapy 4-H club: (1)Hatred, (2)Hurt and (3)Hopelessness. These are, nevertheless, core feelings within our trauma knots.* Feel them (and the fourth H) and the trauma knot will generally be no more. Resist them and the trauma knot will often stay forever. There have been few therapies that attempted to face these feelings directly, Primal Scream Therapy being the most notable example. (Note- real 4-H clubs do superb work with youth and farming/ animals - their four H's are Hands, Head, Heart, and Health.)

Most therapies have attempted to help clients more gently with little or no emphasis on hatred, hurt and hopelessness. The difficulty with *total avoidance* of these painful feelings is that client issues all too frequently never get resolved. They just get managed. For therapists who avoid these H's, cure often becomes a dirty four-letter word because such therapist avoidance makes *resolution* of client issues problematical. The societal benefits would be great if we were all able to face and feel our own H's. But this likely will never happen, for people just will not sign up for the first three H's.

On the other hand, they will sign up for the fourth, Healing. Inner child therapy (i.e., healing the unexpressed words and unfelt feelings of childhood) focuses on Healing, healing the wounded traumatized inner child. In attempting to heal the inner child, the H's of hurt and hopelessness are often faced and felt appropriately. However, it seems to me that the H of Hatred is regularly omitted and overlooked by some of those using inner-child methods with the result that many traumas often do not get resolved.

This chapter will focus upon the four H's: (1)how to recognize them, (2)how to face them, (3)how to feel them and (4)how to get beyond them. While it is theoretically possible for you, the reader, to do this on your own, success is unlikely without some outside help. Also, it may no longer be either necessary or desirable to concentrate on the four H's, for there is a newer therapeutic method that has started revolutionizing trauma work, namely EMDR (Eye Movement Desensitization Reprogramming). The old facing-trauma process could be likened to dentistry without painkillers. Using EMDR, the process is typically eased, smoothed and completed in a much shorter time. If trauma work seems indicated, I highly recommend trying EMDR. It is one of the few methods that produce *resolution* consistently. It is also far less painful than the old-style trauma-facing methods.

BLAMING IS VALUABLE - BLAMING IS USELESS

How can you tell whether the blame you feel is valuable or useless? Many are full of blame these days, blame directed at white males, at black males, at feminists, at government, at fundamentalists, at gays, at the police, at the patriarchy. Those who so blame will seemingly continue to do so until all those being blamed change. Such a 100% perfect result is impossible. Do you enjoy the feeling of everlasting blame? Do you want that feeling for the next 40 years? Such blame keeps the blaming person feeling unhappy. Blame is also often becoming unproductive now in eliciting changes (those blamed frequently feel attacked and defend themselves).

On the other hand, I do consider another type of blame to be valuable. One common feeling within trauma knots is childhood blame, which was often hidden, along with many other feelings and words, at the time of childhood traumas. This blame is directed at someone (usually one or more parenting figures) for not doing "what they should have done" and thus "they caused the trauma." To untie trauma knots it is often useful and productive to blame those parents of yesteryear. The kid within typically needs to blame the parent of yesteryear for the trauma. If that is all that happens, then this type of blame too may never end, for other blocked feelings within the trauma knot must also be felt. If all blocked feelings are felt, then the blame at parents for that particular trauma will end. For the next trauma knot, there will be more childhood blame that can also be resolved by untying enough strands of that next knot.

When clients start upon a course of early-childhood-trauma work with me, I frequently suggest that for about two months that they blame their parents (of many years ago) for all their hangups, all their problems, and all their discomforts. I suggest saying such blaming words only when clients are by themselves or with me, not in person to their parents of today. (Though many do attempt it in person, this results in virtually no success at trauma resolution but sometimes a bit of understanding from the parent of today. Unhappily, the parent of today often denies the validity of the blame.) Best results are often obtained when the blame for a specific problem is voiced aloud to the parent of yesteryear with eyes closed and with a picture of that parent in one's mind: for example, "Mommy, Daddy, you are causing my problem with X." Because most difficulties have their roots in early childhood, such blame is usually accurate and helps to loosen associated childhood trauma knots.

Even today, 23 years after starting my own early childhood therapy work, I sometimes need to blame my parents for a new-to-my-conscious unexplored trauma knot. Such blame usually lasts 15 seconds or less, and then I go on to other aspects of the trauma knot.

Am I Stuck in Blame? If childhood blame for a particular problem persists, it is a clear indicator to me that I am stuck. Any blame I feel about today's life events is also a clear indicator that I am avoiding my own issues. (See next chapter for more on this last statement.) If you, the reader, are stuck, then you may wish to choose to make a new *choice* (see Stage IV in Chapter 4).

We all regularly face the choice to remain stuck or to pursue happier alternatives. This is popularly known as the choice between "being right" and "being happy." This author most definitely recommends dropping the *shoulds* associated with "being right." For self-righteousness alienates others, is often a shaky unstable prop for one's ego, and leads to unhappiness whenever "wrong" ideas/ people/ actions are in view. If self-righteousness or blame of any sort persists, being stuck and being unhappy also persist. To summarize, temporary blame is often essential to the permanent release of trauma knots, whereas blame that persists is clear evidence of being stuck in unhappiness.

HATRED

Many parents would like to believe that their child's hatred is somehow wrong and unnatural. Nevertheless, most children feel it occasionally and are often asked gently or forcibly by their parents to squelch it. Such squelching processes cause significant trauma knots. If parents accepted

If you avoid any specific feeling long enough, it will come to domi-nate you. You will be fearful and live your life as if some shark below were poised to attack. Feel the feeling and that shark disappears.

childhood hatred instead of denigrating it, then it would be expressed and moved beyond without any trauma.

It is my opinion that many therapists who believe hatred to be unimportant are, as a consequence, believers in managing psychological problems rather than resolving them. They often believe that resolution is impossible. I disagree.

An adult who hates his/ her parents of today is clearly indicating skewness of emotional expression. For it is the kid within who hates the parents of many years ago. Therefore, any expression of such rage at the parents of today is skewed and cannot produce resolution of the earlier trauma. In the process of blaming described in preceding paragraphs, it is vital that hatred (the ultimate blaming anger) be felt and expressed by the words "I hate you, Mom/ Dad for .....". So too it may be vital for trauma resolution that kid violent fantasies be felt and expressed in therapy or by oneself, not directly at the hated ones as they are today.

There is a fear that expressing this kid violence will cause violence in today's world. In fact, feeling such kid violence appropriately helps one to become less angry, less violent and much calmer as an adult. It is the denial of such inner kid violence that is one root cause of much of our society's violence*. Our society's increasing acceptance of anger over the past 30 years has brought us all closer to inner-child anger. Because we are closer to it, it erupts more often and in inappropriate ways at today's favorite whipping posts. But to return to our old societal opinion that anger is bad seems ill-advised to this author. Yes, anger and hatred may briefly return when another unexplored traumatic situation is ready to be faced. But their return need only be brief, for the hatred and anger (associated with that previously unexplored traumatic situation) can also be felt and discharged permanently. Hatred and anger can be exorcised and left behind if felt and expressed as suggested in these paragraphs.

HURT

The second core element in trauma knots that is frequently bypassed is that of *hurt* (and its relatives of pain, abandonment, loss, emptiness, depression, dullness, grief, sadness and aloneness). Who really wants to feel these feelings? YOU DO! If you want to move through and beyond your traumas, then these must be felt. You will be forever trying to avoid situations and events that trigger your traumas and the hurts within those traumas if you are unwilling to feel the hurting aspects of being human. It is an unwelcome fact that unwanted situations that trigger our trauma knots will happen despite our efforts at avoidance. Did you know that millions now believe that such avoidance *draws* those unhappy experiences to us? (See next chapter.)

Am I stuck in hurt? If I am hurt a lot by current events in my life, I am probably stuck trying to avoid childhood hurts (or other elements of trauma knots, particularly hatred). If feeling my hurt doesn't ease it and eventually eliminate it, then I am stuck. *If I still feel hurt by any past experience, then I have therapy work to do.*

Frequently the operative words of the inner child that help move us through hurt feelings are "You hurt me when you....". Such words often bring us immediately into our feelings of grief, which will often be enough to release a trauma knot permanently, particularly if the hatred about that trauma has already been felt.

HOPELESSNESS

The third core element in trauma knots that usually must be faced is *hopelessness*. The strategy that one has been employing to avoid the trauma is clearly seen to be hopeless. The struggle to please Mom and Dad is seen as hopeless. The struggle to please others today will never produce the love that one needed when the struggle was adopted so long ago. Once this hopelessness is felt, then the urge to go one's own way is often easily followed.

One crucial psychological problem confronting disadvantaged African-Americans seems to me to be that of hopelessness. "This is a bigoted society that stacks all the cards against me. There is no way I can get ahead." Such difficulties with hopelessness are often compounded by the following belief in entitlement: "In whatever ways I feel bad, the government/ society should fix." The fact that the chances of an African-American with a B+ or better average getting to college are better than the chances of whites being admitted needs to be broadcast widely by the media. Many African-American parents feel much hopelessness. Just knowing this fact (Bennett 1992, 196) about college availability would change a significant amount of hopelessness and would lead parents to be far more demanding of their children in terms of grades. Parents <u>know</u> a B+ average is easily possible for most high-school students, whatever their skin color. Feeling hopeless about society can also obscure a crucial need to feel hopeless concerning one's own parents.

Most everyone would do well to face their own childhood hopelessness concerning their own parents. ***This hopelessness stage is characterized by tears*** *and grief.* It is a difficult stage that we all tend to avoid, because it usually requires that we have faced all the unhappy, unsettling, denied feelings within the trauma knot under consideration. Happily, it is a stage of resolution.

HEALING

An important truth is that the body reacts virtually the same way to an imagined experience as it does to a real experience.* This phenomenon has been used recently by many therapists to provide some corrective childhood experiences for the 97% of us who suffered traumas back then. If I didn't get enough holding from Dad, then I can imagine that I am 3 or 11 pretending all sorts of experiences where Dad of yesteryear holds me lovingly. By such a process I can provide myself significant healing of my old needing-Dad's-love trauma. If it is too difficult to imagine your particular parents being so different, then you can create two new imaginary parents for yourself. (I think it less productive if you imagine yourself as an adult holding the child-you. If the exercise is done in this manner, many don't feel the full force of the available healing. Because it is a useful first step for some, however, try it if you cannot imagine yourself being the small child getting the healing.)

Such healing work has been made well known by John Bradshaw. The below list of healing statements is suggested. The first five are from *Homecoming* (Bradshaw 1992, 93). The remainder come from this author.

Healing Work

It will probably be most effective if you say these ten statements aloud into your tape recorder. Then listen to them with closed eyes, and imagine yourself as a baby/ toddler being held by and told these words by a loving parent:

"Welcome to the world, I've been waiting for you."

"I will not leave you, no matter what."

"I like feeding you, bathing you, changing you and spending time with you."

"I'm so glad you're a boy (or a girl)."

"God smiled when you were born."

I want you to enjoy your entire body, your lips, your mouth, your stomach, your fingers, your genitals and your toes- your entire body.

I'll come whenever you need me.

It's OK to be angry or sad.

I love you just the way you are.

I love holding you, cuddling you and stroking you. I love you, my little one.

If this type of healing seems right for you, then there are many more healing ways described in *Homecoming*. The more you practice being the child who gets the love rather than being the adult who gives it to the child-you, the more effective such work will likely be.

THE FUTURE

This mythical Therapy 4-H Club will never be joined by many (even in spirit) and is basically no longer really necessary. The new therapeutic method mentioned earlier, EMDR, will do the same job on trauma more quickly and effectively than any of the older methods with which I am acquainted. While the fourth H, Healing, may still be used regularly, the first three H's will likely only be encountered briefly in the course of EMDR treatment sessions. They still may need to be faced, but not with as much pain and distress as was required to effect trauma resolution via old-style therapeutic methods.**

This chapter may have shown you where you are stuck in trauma resolution. Each client and each therapist usually have specific H's that are consistently avoided. Just knowing which H is missing will often be enough to propel you toward its resolution.

*Healing of traumas today is much
easier and less painful than ever before.*

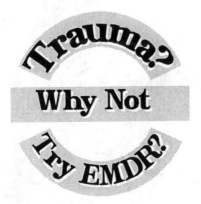

---

* See Appendix A

**Possible additions to your I-WANT-LIST (see Appendix C):
        I want to allow myself my hatreds.
        I want to try healing by means of healing statements given earlier in this chapter.
        I want to heal my traumas via EMDR.

Many politicians, doctors, lawyers and politically-correct organizations are shouting in your ear:

Don't Read This Chapter!!

Chapter 11

Spirituality

(9 do not mean religion!)

Note: This chapter has the potential for many readers to give you more "bang for the buck" (i.e., more happiness for you from a minimum of effort) than any other chapter in this book.

WAS THIS CHAPTER BANNED IN BOSTON?

Banning in Boston does seem remote, given modern Boston and this chapter's lack of sexual content. Nevertheless, there are many powerful interest groups who might prefer that you skipped this chapter: politicians, doctors, lawyers, insurance companies, the cultural elite, clergy, hospitals, funeral directors, also many organizations that are politically and socially *correct*. Why? All the above organizational groups might lose money and power if many of us changed in ways suggested by this chapter. The results of much improved happiness and autonomy for each of us (black, white, straight, gay, male or female) might not be appreciated by the above interest groups!

As noted above, this chapter has the potential for more resulting happiness from less effort than any other chapter in this book. Wouldn't you like to gain some serenity about things like severe trauma, debilitating injuries and death? Wouldn't you prefer to be less concerned with materialistic worries? Wouldn't you prefer to feel safe, rather than terrorized?

GOLDEN RETREIVER MAGIC

One July night I dreamed of a severed dog leg, lying on the ground. My older golden retriever Pol, then 11 years old, had legs the approximate size, shape and color of the severed leg in my dream. "That age is near the end of a normal golden retriever life-span," the vet had told me two weeks before my dream. With my knowledge of the old Freudian idea (not 100% correct in my opinion) that all dreams are just wish fulfillment, the dream was not easy to tolerate. After much introspection, I really found no wish on my part for either of my two dogs to be injured or dead. So I let the matter remain in doubt.

Eight weeks later, while taking my two retrievers along the beach for a September ocean swim, a three-legged Irish Setter was headed toward us. The shoulder wound associated with his missing leg was as might be expected after eight weeks of healing. Also, this Irish Setter was strongly emotionally wounded. He visibly drooped and exhibited a hangdog look that clearly said that life did not seem worth living for him. Surprisingly, my dogs, Pol and Tash, approached him individually and somewhat calmly, instead of making their typical boisterous joint charge toward other canines. Within the space of two minutes of dog-sniffing and circling, it was obvious that the Irish Setter's feelings had changed from "Life-is-not-living" to "Ain't life grand?". The woman with the Irish Setter, whom I had never before met, just said two words to me, "Thank you." We then parted.

So what happened? Some may think it was a random chance that I dreamed of a severed dog leg about the time of the Irish Setter's accident. On the other hand, the half of this country's population now believing in ESP would be of a different opinion. ESP and precognition, rather than amazing coincidence, seem better explanations for my dream at the time of the Irish Setter's accident (two months before we were all to meet). To doubters- do you really think my dream was coincidence? To believers- yes, I know I left out talk of the probable agreements between the woman and myself.

P.S. For another four years my two dogs and I lived happily together without injury to either one of them.

SPIRITUALITY - TRUTH OR QUACKERY?

Spirituality is defined as "life and consciousness away from the body" (*Oxford* 1980, s.v. "spirituality"). This definition can be useful, for it neither implies nor denies the presence of some organized religion. Is there life or consciousness away from our bodies? If so, what is it? Can we experience some of it without being commanded to "take it on faith?"

Popular literature recently has been full of discussions of such matters, from out-of-body experiences to near-death experiences to past lives regression therapy. Is this all hocus-pocus or is there truth among the many claims?

You may believe that we are just our bodies and that our consciousness dies with our bodies. Such a belief causes distress (life at all costs is one major area of distress caused by such a belief). There are many opportunities in today's world to experience something different.* One possibility for a different experience is to seek some OBE (out-of-body experience) by studying Monroe's *Journeys Out of The Body*, a classic work about OBEs. To play with projecting your consciousness elsewhere, you can try the spoon-bending mentioned later in this chapter. Or talk with someone who has had a near-death experience (you have heard about it - the tunnel, the white light and looking back at the body). You could also try to reach your past lives' experience via hypnosis, also described later in this chapter. The above are just some of the current opportunities for *direct experience* of your spirituality. Are you afraid of such direct experience? Most find such experiences fun. Why not try right now for the fun of Appendix F, *The Ouija Board for Psychic Klutzes?*

SPIRITUALITY IS NOT RELIGION

The above definition of spirituality, "life and consciousness away from the body," implies the existence of spirit or soul. Very different implications arise from the first (*Oxford* 1980) dictionary definition of *religion*, "belief in the existence of a superhuman controlling power....usually expressed in worship". Worship implies that whoever is doing the worshiping is not as good as the god being worshiped. It also usually results in clergy, priests, ministers or leaders who gain power over worshipers by claims of superior knowledge.

After the death of a religion's great spiritual leader, it is common for followers to develop hierarchies and rules that are far removed from the teachings of that leader. These rules tend to promote the hierarchy in preference to the teaching. It seems to me that the fundamental words and teachings of the greats like Lao-Tzu, Buddha, Mohammed and Jesus are as valid today as when those men walked the planet. However, the followers running the religious hierarchies resulting from those teachers have often interpreted the original teachings to suit the hierarchy. This, of course, often radically alters the original teachings. If your religion sticks closely to the original words of these leaders and discards words of other less important prophets/ teachers where they conflict with the teachings of the great teachers, then it is probable that you have a religion that permits you happiness. If not, then it is helpful to remember that *faith*, not religion, is usually the crucible that permits happiness to florish.

It remains popular today among a few of the better educated to hold the Marxist belief that "religion is the opium of the people." That does seem true for some sects of the more strident variety, but lumping all spiritual and religious systems together without closer examination does not seem particularly intelligent to me. By taking this judgmental position, such people seem to be throwing out the baby along with the bath-water.

With my clients I am often a sales agent for spirituality (any happiness-permitting variety). For without some sense of or belief in one's spiritual nature, (1)we miss much real satisfaction in life and (2)we retain much unhappiness in perpetuity. For more information, I recommend consulting healing-spirituality pioneer Dr. M. Scott Peck's *The Road Less Traveled.* In my therapy office I often dialog with clients about their unhappy spiritual beliefs, particularly those that preach hatred and condemnation of others. Condemnation of others seems to violate the words of most great founders of religion (Jesus, Lao-Tzu, Buddha and Mohammed).

WHEN DOES RANDOM CHANCE BECOME A FRAUD?

This author has a significant background in the sciences, studying about probabilities in college, also several years teaching nuclear reactor technology in the Navy's nuclear propulsion program. Nowhere in the undergraduate or postgraduate instruction I received did I hear of any difficulties with theories about randomness. Most branches of science depend heavily upon the concept of randomness. According to randomness theory it is a 50-50 random chance whether the coin I flip turns up heads or tails. This can be "proved" by all sorts of experiments.

Now let the human mind and/or consciousness start to become involved in so-called random chance events. Scientists have completed studies in this area. For example, set up an experiment in which a human subject guesses which one of five shapes is on the back of a card. The results are startling to those believing in random chance. Some people regularly and routinely far exceed the 20% success rate one would expect. Further, they are as capable even if the experiment is rearranged so that no one, not even the experimenter, knows what is on the back of a given card during the test.

Spoon-bending is a widely demonstrated example of how the human conscious mind can influence outside objects (projection of consciousness). A group of people gather, each with a cheap metal spoon in hand and strongly focus their conscious intent upon bending their spoons. Lo and behold, most of the spoons bend like putty and/or are significantly warmed at the narrow bending point (The bending point is not where the hand holds the spoon.) This seems rarely to work for one person, but for many gathered with strong visualized intention, the result is many bent spoons. According to theories of randomness, even one spoon bending in such a fashion carries almost zero probability. To have it happen predictably "must be fraud."

Fun Growth Exercise. Instead of instantly calling spoon-bending "nothing but a fraud," I suggest attending such a spoon-bending party. Or throw your own party if you know of no others in your vicinity. What do you have to lose except some old cobwebs in the brain?

For decades "strange" and "bizarre" results have appeared in physics experiments that concern themselves with small waves or particles. Explanations for these results have proven elusive, even with accepted theories such as "uncertainty principles." Such "bizarreness" has been a thorn in the sides of those in the scientific community.

Perhaps a "bizarre" (to conventional scientists) theory might explain these strange results. Consider the possibility that randomness theory is like Newton's theory, valid only up to a point. The monkey wrench in Newton's theory arises when speeds approach that of light. Then Einstein's theories require alterations in Newton's formulas. In terms of randomness, it is my belief that the monkey wrench in randomness theory arises when there is *significant* conscious (and/or unconscious) intent. Such intent seems to significantly alter the situation and often overrides mathematical probabilities and randomness formulas.

EARTH SCHOOL

One basic question that each of us must answer is, "What is the meaning of life?" Your answer to that question has much relevance to your

It Is Difficult to Make a Man Miserable While He Feels Worthy of Himself and Claims Kindred to the Great God Who Made Him.

Abraham Lincoln

ability to be happy.* Many of us don't have solid convictions about the meaning of life and have uncritically adopted conventional wisdom expressed by those around us. There are many different answers to that meaning-of-life question, some of which automatically cause much distress and unhappiness. Other answers to the question allow for (but do not necessarily automatically result in) contentment and happiness.

The one common ingredient in answers that *will* allow contentment is what I call the belief in Earth School. Specifically, we all attend Earth School here on this planet for learning various things. The spiritual systems that seem to permit inner peace are those that include the belief that one major meaning of life is to learn about: oneself (body, mind, emotions and soul), the world around us, choice, relationships, values, service and a few of the myriad facets of life about which we are ignorant. On some levels most of the major religions subscribe to this belief. But following any religion, whether organized or unorganized, is not necessary to gain the benefits from such a belief.

Earth School Beliefs

(1)Earth School routinely gives me demanding challenges/lessons my conscious self would prefer to avoid.

(2)Whatever challenges/lessons are thrown my way in life are always there to teach me something.

(3)I can choose to follow my old ways and suffer, or I can choose to change myself (ideas, emotions and/or body) to master the challenges/ lessons being offered me.

All three of the above beliefs are somewhat unpopular these days. Three popular ideas follow. (1)Randomness and being the victim are correct. Therefore it is not possible that there are some important higher powers and meanings involved in the creation of challenging life events. (2)If I can be politically-correct and blame someone else, then I don't have to face myself. Therefore, I refuse to believe that life's challenges are there to teach me something. (3)I blame the handiest outside person or group for my distress, waiting for them to change so that I can finally be happy (which doesn't happen because *all* those being blamed never do change).

Please reread the previous paragraph. It contains the root causes of much of our unhappiness as a society today. For if we could change our society's thinking away from that in the last paragraph, the improvements would be quite dramatic for all. Changing society involves changing individuals first. Do your beliefs need changing?

To resolve our distress here on Earth School, it must be moved through, not avoided or blamed on someone/ something else. Moving through distress is initially more difficult than trying to avoid it, but avoidance only works temporarily (like the addict's fix).

HAPPIER CHOICES

A middle-aged client one day was expressing her anger to me about her mild birth defect, which somewhat limited her physically. Part of my response to her was that choosing a new spiritual system was likely to be essential if she were to eliminate the anger.* Obviously, I was confronting rather than being empathic with her conscious mind then. For the empathy of friends, therapists, support groups and her spouse in the past had not helped to change that anger. She needed the belief that the birth defect, instead of being something that "should not have happened," was a positive life challenge for her to overcome and move beyond.

The challenge for her was to feel OK with her physical condition, to accept it and its limitations without anger, regret, sadness or angst of any kind. Her spiritual beliefs were based upon the common "What we get in life is random chance" belief and the so-called "scientific" belief that when our body dies, our mind does also. Her beliefs caused this woman (1)to be forever angry at how unfair it was to be so randomly selected for a disability and (2)to feel forever cheated because she would never experience a normal body. Happier choices were available to her:

(1)A religious system in which God gives out such defects for reasons known only to God is potentially a happy belief system.

(2)A system such as Buddhism or Hinduism in which reincarnation and perhaps karma play vital roles would give her the faith that she would have other lifetimes with a normal body.

(3)A system that espouses a Higher Power (perhaps one's higher self or God) who gives out such problems as challenges to overcome could prove to be a path of contentment.

(4) Any other belief system, in which one vital meaning of life is that this is Earth School for her, would be a potentially satisfying belief system. This schooling could be learning about overcoming disability, learning about people, learning how to overcome poor self-esteem or childhood abuse, learning how to love, also learning in the more traditional areas of reading, social studies, etc.

If she (my client with a mild birth defect) chose any of the above belief systems, then happiness was possible. But it would require changing herself! (She <u>had</u> already accomplished much in therapy before ever coming to me.) It feels so much safer to blame life or others for our discomforts. We feel so self-righteous. The problem is out there, not with us. For anyone who is likely to be permanently different, (differences might include physical disability, skin color, ethnic background, religious orientation or sexual inclination), the standard USA beliefs of random chance and one-time-around will result in perpetual unhappiness. In fact, all of us are different from the majority in many ways because there really is no majority these days. If we persist in being unhappy about our differences from others, it is our responsibility to change ourselves. If we don't change, we glue ourselves to perpetual unhappiness.

TWO HAPPIER BELIEF SYSTEMS

There are two happier spiritual belief systems available that have neither the trappings of organized Western religions nor the "foreign" flavor of the East. They are not organized religions, groups or cults. They are channeled systems of beliefs couched in language with which you and I are likely to be comfortable. The first is the Michael teaching as described in *Messages from Michael* by Chelsea Yarbro. The second is the Seth teaching as described in *Seth Speaks* and *The Nature of Personal Reality*, both by Jane Roberts. (These authors' early books listed above had best be read first because their later books can be confusing if attempted first.) Either of these two systems has the potential for transforming unhappy areas of your life into contented areas.

I sometimes lend a copy of the Michael book to people suggesting they read only as much as necessary to figure out if they want to spend the money to buy their own copy. I sometimes jokingly refer to the Michael book as "Spirituality for the Masses" to give people an idea of how down-to-earth the book really is. It is not esoteric. While some object to its belief system, calling it rigid or simplistic, many more come to see its value and to realize that its categories are tendencies, not rigid prescriptions. Any of the above three listed books can explain worlds to someone who is open to such explanation. You may rest assured that no one will be at your door Saturday morning proselytizing about them! Too simplistically - the Michael system explains tendencies we have, whereas the Seth system explains how our reality is created by each of us.

For many of you readers, one of the most important growth exercises you could do would be to find and read one or more of the above three books. What do you have to lose, other than much of your unhappiness? If these books sound at all interesting, take some action.

ONE-TIME-AROUND VS. REINCARNATION

While current polls show only about 25% of the USA population believes in reincarnation, the USA belief in one-time-around is actually a minority world view. And the one-time-around view can lead to much unhappiness and spinning of wheels, particularly for the following groups of people: women, minorities, never-married, "victims" of natural or manmade events and those of alternate sexual persuasions. The above groups will tend to think this an unjust world if they believe in one-time-around and remain focused upon the outside "injustices" rather than working to change themselves so that they move beyond Stage II *blame* (see Chapter 4 for information about stages of healing).

Knowledge of one's previous lives, which is available to virtually everyone via hypnosis, automatically changes one's perspective. The disabled and chronically ill discover that such difficulties are usually only for a lifetime or two out of many. A macho male may discover a wimpy female or gay lifetime. The feminist may discover that last time around she was a man who thought women were scum. Gays and lesbians discover they were homophobic heterosexuals in other lifetimes. African-Americans discover white lives, also black lives as the majority race. Caucasians discover lives as blacks. Parents whose children die young discover long lives with such children in earlier times. Such knowledge of prior lives changes one's current beliefs and one's feelings about this life's problems and difficulties. Acceptance is a frequent result. This acceptance does not lead to inaction but to taking much more effective action to change one's current situation.

The history of beliefs in reincarnation goes back to the dawn of time and was even present in several early Christian teachings. Then, during the Dark Ages, the Catholic Church decided that such beliefs did not help to promote the authority of the clergy or the church. Why pay that much attention to my clergyman if I'll just cycle through again no matter whether I follow what he says or not? Why fear hell and damnation if I just come back here to earth if I fail to do it right this time around? One would expect that clergy concerned with their own power and influence over their followers would come to consider the idea of reincarnation to be extremely sacrilegious. So they did. The words of Christ, as written in the gospels, however, seem to neither condemn nor approve the idea. The topic apparently is not mentioned. In the tradition of Judaism, on the other hand, there has been significant approval of the idea of reincarnation. And, of course, major Eastern religions such as Hinduism and Buddhism have reincarnation as an integral part of their beliefs.

The question is always raised, "If I had those lives, why don't I remember them?". That question can be answered as follows: if this is Reincarnational Earth School, where for our advanced degree we need to experience different sides of the same experience (such as man/woman, gay/straight, black/white, cynic/idealist, expressive/retentive), then we would have too much knowledge of the opposite experience if we remembered prior lives. Therefore, our other lives need to be generally shielded from us. Questions often are raised too about the increasing population on this earth. Reincarnationists have explained this by saying (1)that new souls continue to come into our system, (2)that our higher selves can have more than one soul here at a time, and (3)that we are now coming back more often with less time between incarnations. (This last point was corroborated by Helen Wambach's research in *Reliving Past Lives: The Evidence from Hypnosis.*) A major objection to beliefs in reincarnation comes from the scientific community, which "doesn't see any past lives." Most scientists haven't looked very hard and tend to discount even their own members who have some personal experience. To them, this author says, "Try it and then see if you are still a non-believer." My *direct* experience has led me to the opposite opinion about reincarnation from the opinion I had when I was making my living as a nuclear engineer many years ago.

The advantages to believing in one-time-around are: (1)that I can feel the comfort of being in the majority of this society (small comfort) and (2)that it allows me to be a perpetually unhappy helpless victim who never has to assume responsibility for my own happiness. I don't want that for myself. Do you?

Yes, there is garbage astrology out there. But finding the astrological baby and discarding the bath-water is not that difficult.

PAST LIVES THERAPY

Doesn't such a therapy sound esoteric and mystical? It really isn't that way 99% of the time. The experience is more like eating thick soup - solid, real and satisfying (but not dull). For several years there have been therapists who have been using hypnosis to regress people to past life experiences. A solid informative book on the subject has been published recently, *Through Mind into Healing* by Dr. Brian Weiss. While only a minority of clients seem to be in need of this type of therapy, it usually resolves issues that have never before been amenable to resolution with other more conventional therapies.

Personally I first experienced past lives regression in a 1980s classroom experiment with other prospective psychotherapists. It was a big surprise then to discover that I was a different sex when I "looked down at my body in my mind's eye" as directed by the hypnotist. The solid details are what make such an experience feel so real: the type of shoes being worn, the old-fashioned money, the worn bench and most especially, the ordinariness of it all. Several years later I sought out a therapist who did past lives therapy. I discovered in that therapy that in a prior lifetime I had died giving birth to a child. That explained much of my discomfort then with my own sexuality, trauma knots from that lifetime affecting me in this lifetime. (There will be those reading this who "know" that it was trauma in this lifetime that I was avoiding. No. I disagree. I entered past lives therapy after years of primal therapy, a therapy that focused exclusively on this lifetime's traumas. Primal treatment had done little up to then to ease that discomfort.)

> **Growth Exercise.** Find a hypnotist who does past life regressions and try it out for yourself. You don't have to do therapy. Just find out what there is to see and experience.

While resolving trauma in this lifetime may take months or even years, resolving the effects of past life trauma knots on this lifetime is usually much quicker. Insight will often be sufficient. If not, and the trauma knot in a past life must be faced, its knotting effect on this life usually gets untied more readily than if it were this life's trauma knot.

Whether the idea of past lives is The Truth is just not that important. For as more than one fellow therapist told Dr. Weiss (Weiss 1992, 55), "I still don't know if I believe in this past life stuff, but I use it, and it sure does work!"

I

ASTROLOGY

Is your immediate response to astrology "what claptrap!"? Please read on. I vividly remember a phone conversation with an old friend. He and I had spent much time together during the years when I was strongly involved with nuclear propulsion, radiological controls, reactor physics, sonar, thermodynamics, heat transfer, pressure-vessel design and duplicate bridge. After not talking with that friend for several years, we talked by telephone one afternoon. During the conversation I playfully mentioned something astrological, perhaps something like, "Maybe your moon is in Aquarius." He was shocked that I had come to believe in such foolishness. He obviously thought that my mind was going soft and that I should discard such bath-water concepts. However, I think it is more a question of separating the astrological baby from the bath-water than labeling everything bath-water.

In my opinion, you will not find the astrological baby in the daily/ weekly/ monthly columns or in the yearly books published for your birth sign. I would agree that those sources of information are mostly bath-water. Your birth chart, on the other hand, typically does give useful information about trends and tendencies you naturally possess.

Fun Growth Exercise. Get your astrological birth chart done, complete with conjunctions, oppositions, squares and trines. Consult a thick text such as Sakoian and Acker's *The Astrologer's Handbook* on how to interpret those conjunctions et al. In almost all cases those who try this exercise will discover that the interpretations are far more accurate than would be expected from anything that was wholly bath-water.

Astrology shows influences, tendencies and likelihoods. If we choose, we always can go against these predilections, usually to our significant pain and discomfort. Reincarnation ideas fit astrology very well, for the astrological birth chart reveals Earth School lessons that have been chosen for this lifetime. There will not be 100% accuracy, perhaps only 50% accuracy, because astrology shows tendencies not the actual outcome. But the experience of that 50% accuracy usually boggles the minds of unbelievers. It often changes their minds about the validity of astrological information. Your birth chart shows lessons for your entire life. Therefore, part of it will not be accurate today but was correct yesterday or will be correct in your future.

Also, I have found the transits of the outer planets to the birth chart to be amazingly accurate in terms of predicting *when and in what areas* significant life choices and life events will occur. But as a predictor of exactly *what* will happen, I have not found astrology to be particularly useful unless the astrologer is also a competent psychic who can tune into probable future events. (If the future depends at least partially upon decisions we make between now and then, psychics will always have a few errors in their predictions.)

Most of us imprinted ourselves during our growing-up years with many of our parents' ideas, tendencies and predilections. They are not our own. Typically as teenagers we start to tune into and follow our own. This teen psychological growth process is typically incomplete, often because of unexplored trauma knots. Many people have found that astrology gives them important insights into their unconscious predilections and their unexamined parental imprinting. These insights lead them to significantly less distress and discomfort in their lives, because they then can follow their own true inclinations and stop the slavish following of unexamined parental views.

THIS IS A SAFE UNIVERSE

Do the words "this is a safe universe" resonate negatively with you? In this culture, a poll would probably reveal that negative responses to that statement predominated. Yet such a belief is precisely the one that can lead to incredible freedom to follow one's own path with inner trust and confidence.* Without it, one is always looking over one's shoulder for the next disaster, which "surely must be coming since this is an unsafe universe."

To come to believe the world is safe, it is particularly useful to have had the *experience* of "my body is not all of me." Therefore, there has been significant emphasis in this chapter on experiences that show us that our consciousness does not depend upon the body for its existence. (I have included experiences such as near-death, out-of-body, regression to past lives, spoon-bending, etc.) Such experiences lead us toward the realization that we are more consciousness than corporal. Of course our bodies die, but that in no way means that consciousness dies. To truly believe that one's consciousness does not die is very freeing.

We have all been heavily trained to believe that this is an unsafe world, particularly as children but also as adults. To shake the effects of that training will usually take time and many conscious realizations along the lines of "I just slipped back into those old fears." When that happens, it helps to repeat to oneself five times, "this is a safe universe."

> *Spirit Is the Real
> and Eternal; Matter
> is......Temporal.*
> *Mary Baker Eddy*

I GET EXACTLY WHAT I NEED

A very freeing (and at times incredibly challenging) belief is: *there are reasons why I get each life problem and challenge.* Whatever the universe gives me in terms of benefits, disasters, people, losses, challenges, money and diseases are in my life for reasons specific to me. They are there now because I need them there now. They are the best possible teachers for me here on Earth School now.

These days my friends and I often jokingly call our upsets and disasters "more #$&*@ growth opportunities." This *does* imply that there is a higher power or god or unconscious part of ourselves who/ which knows what we need and is arranging it. (Our conscious minds would never go along with selecting many of the disasters.) Whatever discomforts we get, they are there to spur our growth and change, not to be blamed upon so-called "perpetrators". (Not that it wouldn't be beneficial for the "perpetrators" to change. But if they change before we accomplish the growth they are providing us the opportunity for, then we will probably just manifest new "perpetrators" into our lives so that we may accomplish our needed growth.) It often is anything but a simple process to change our responses to these #$&*@ growth opportunities. Such change can take anywhere from a few moments to years.

Caution: Others in the midst of some disaster will not appreciate your words describing how perfect the disaster is for them! They will need to feel and express in their own ways, whatever those ways may be. It is *later,* when they appear stuck, (and have already expressed many words and feelings about the experience), that the possibility arises to gently ask about the positive learning side of what has happened. Your most effective communication with them will depend upon their spiritual belief systems. Few in this culture believe in the perfection of who they are and of what they get. Therefore, the best questions are often, "What is the positive side of this?" or "What have you learned from this?" If you are communicating with a reincarnation believer or a strong believer in a particular religion, on the other hand, questions about their learning or about the perfection of a disaster can be asked much earlier.

Please note the complete lack of victim mentality in the statement, *I get exactly what I need.* The challenge is to move through a problem so that it is no longer a problem rather than remain stuck in feeling victimized. If someone in my life is doing something that causes me significant distress, then my challenge is most often not to stop them but to change my responses so that the next time I will not be adversely affected. Challenging? Yes! But I have retained my power (and part of the exercise of my power may be to move out of unhealthy circumstances). If my happiness depends upon them changing, then I have given away my power. When some discomfort or disaster arises, believing absolutely in its necessity for me will lead me to the new learning I need now. Then, when I have learned the lesson(s), the discomfort will ease.

WHAT ABOUT BEING A VICTIM?

Why are you questioning me so? Didn't I suffer many traumas as a child at the hands of parents who drank, fought a lot, and failed to meet my emotional needs? *Yes.*

What about the disasters I have suffered as an adult because of others? Wasn't I a victim then or when I was a child? *That depends upon what you believe. Ultimately you will be happier if you believe your higher self chose your parents and all those disastrous experiences as lessons this time around on Earth School.*

Few in this culture (probably fewer than 10% of the population) would agree with the statement, "there are no victims." That statement initially seems harsh, uncaring and offensive. But belief in its validity will free the believer in many ways. Holding such a belief does require assuming a load, that of responsibility for one's contentment. Such a load is not a burden, but an adventure. To believe my higher self does know what I need and is giving it to me, however much my conscious self objects, is empowering.

SUMMARY OF BELIEFS HAPPY AND UNHAPPY

Just knowing which of the below beliefs are happy and which are unhappy can give you a boost down the change path. Once you have reread the applicable section(s) of this book, you will need to read other books for more detail concerning these happy/ unhappy beliefs .**

Happy Beliefs	Unhappy Beliefs
There is meaning to life.	Life has no meaning.
My consciousness is eternal.	My consciousness dies with my body.
Intent can alter probabilities.	Probabilities don't depend upon thoughts.
This is Earth School.	Events in my life aren't there for a reason.
There is no blame.	It is important to blame correctly.
My disability is there for a reason.	My physical disability is unjust.
Any reincarnational system.	One time around.
I get exactly what I need.	I am a victim.
This is a safe world/ universe.	This world is unsafe.

*Changing a few beliefs (such as the
preceding happy/ unhappy beliefs) is often
the fastest way to feelings of
solid happiness and life satisfaction.*

---

* See Appendix A

**Possible additions to your I-WANT-LIST (see Appendix C):
    I want to change one belief (see previous page) to a happy one. Which?
    I want to read one of the following (see bibliography for publishing details):.
        Journeys Out of the Body
        Messages from Michael
        Seth Speaks
        The Nature of Personal Reality
        Through Mind into Healing
        The Road Less Traveled

This author wants <u>you</u>!

Chapter 12

Our Favorite Groups Have Problems Too

THIS AUTHOR WANTS <u>YOU!</u>

During WWII there was a famous poster of Uncle Sam pointing his finger at the camera saying, "Uncle Sam Wants You." The poster obviously attempted to get the observer to make the difficult choice to sign up for the military. I am attempting something similar, trying to deepen your personal involvement with the difficult issues in this book. Up to now, many readers (you, too?) have been reading glibly along without fully accepting that I really did mean <u>them</u> when I discussed difficult issues. These next chapters, in which I talk controversially about your favorite groups, will leave you in no doubt that I really did mean you too. Your reaction may take several forms:

(1) You can blame me, thereby keeping yourself in Stage II unhappiness (see Chapter 4 for description of Stages).
(2) You can decide that change is necessary for you and decide upon waiting, Stage III, or what new choice, Stage IV, is appropriate for you now.
(3) You can decide I am wrong and *happily* choose to read further, or you can choose to drop this book for now/ forever.

Obviously, (2) and (3) are happier choices than (1).

CELEBRATION TIME

Historically, a generation or more ago, this society was in Stage I *denial* about many things, most particularly the effects of sexist, racist and anti-gay opinions. For these opinions negatively affected our whole society, including those so voicing such pejorative opinions. As groups of women,

135

African-Americans and gays became more aware, they tended to stop Stage I *denying* and start into Stage II *blaming*. Angry demonstrations, civil disobedience and faultfinding of others were and are the manifestations of this blaming. This worked to change millions of us! A vital question to ask is, "How far have we come?" The answer is, "We <u>have</u> come a long way, baby, and not just women." All major societal groups have changed significantly in the past 50 years, much more than commonly thought.

The essential definition of sexism is that one sex feels superior to another, and similarly the belief that one race is inherently superior to another defines racism. Being anti-gay implies a judgment that gays are not OK. So how many believe today they are superior to women/ blacks or that gays are not OK? **A minority!** Instead of the wide majority who believed those things 50 years ago, perhaps fewer than 20% today believe they are inherently a superior gender, a superior race or the only OK sexual orientation. This means that 80% of the population is not, according to strict definition, sexist, racist or anti-gay. Doesn't that strike you as cause for celebration? We **have** come a long way. We do have the makings for a rather harmonious society because of these changes. I believe things really are much better than what is being promulgated by all the Stage II blamers. Later I'll discuss more about how to do what remains to be done, but please celebrate *now* what we have accomplished!

Celebration Time

If we are such a sexist society why do men vote as much as they do for women candidates? If we are such a racist society, why do blacks with a B+ average have a better chance than whites of entering college?

MUST LACK OF UNDERSTANDING FEEL BAD?

When someone doesn't understand us and without any awareness walks over our feelings, most of us feel at least a twinge of discomfort. The real problem is that almost all our childhood trauma knots are triggered when we are not understood. If our families had <u>understood</u> back then, they would have done things differently and prevented most of our psychological traumas. Therefore, any perceived lack of understanding in the present triggers the pain and stress associated with childhood trauma knots we have yet untied.

But is this automatic, to become unhappy when someone doesn't understand us? If a native from the jungle doesn't understand us, we are not bothered. Therefore our unhappiness is not automatic, for it depends upon our expectations. If we can let go the expectations for others to understand us, then we will not be bothered when they do misunderstand. Isn't it foolish to expect understanding from so many? We rarely have even one or two people in our lives who even seem close to understanding us fully. To expect those with very different upbringings to understand us just causes us unhappiness. And it is not necessary, if we can let go our expectations for them. Millions of men, women, blacks, whites, straights and gays are caught in this understanding trap, expecting our opposites to understand. They will never fully understand, for their life experiences have been very different. (Nor do we understand them as well as we have led ourselves to believe.)

> <u>**Getting Out of the I-Need-You-to-Understand Trap.**</u> The first key is to accept that it is possible to not be bothered by others' lack of understanding. Then, repeat the following statements to yourself five times whenever you are triggered by others' lack of understanding: "I don't need their understanding" and "Of course they don't understand. Their life experiences have been very different from mine." (If you are capable of resolving traumas a la Chapter 10, then that is another possible method of extricating yourself from this trap.)

It has been extremely popular recently for lack of understanding to be given the incorrect labels of sexism, racism and homophobia. To those so using the labels incorrectly this author shouts, "Cease and desist!"

> <u>**Exercise for Those Frequently Using the Words *Sexism, Racism* or *Homophobia.***</u> The first time you use one of those words, pat yourself on the back. The next eleven times you use it, take the following three

Its name is Public
Opinion. It is held in rever-
ence. It settles everything.
Some think it is the voice
of God.
Mark Twain 1925

steps: (1)take a wooden 12-inch ruler in your right hand and rap the knuckles of your left hand, (2)then using your left hand, raise your right foot to your mouth and insert foot, and finally, (3)look up as eleven cream pies hit you in the face.

Somehow, I don't think you did the above exercise. But my intent was to use the humor in hopes that you, the reader, would associate something different with the words sexism, racism and homophobia. Perhaps you will think of a cream pie in the face when you are next tempted to use such a word. For I believe that the current overuse of such buzzwords is *now* having deleterious effects upon the goals of women, blacks and gays. In the initial stages of change, it was very helpful to use such words, but today we are no longer in those initial stages of societal change.

Where misunderstanding is the real issue, just calling it "misunderstanding" will promote dialogue with the 80% of the population who aren't claiming gender/ racial/ sexual superiority. That friendly 80% *know* they aren't racist, sexist or anti-gay for they have thought about such issues, looked inside themselves and found no belief in innate superiority. Blaming and pejorative labels today often just alienate that friendly 80% and will not change the rigid 20% who retain their old sexist/ racist/ anti-gay ideas.

Hard Truths About

UNDERSTANDING AND BEING UNDERSTOOD

1. We do not understand each other well, and that is OK.

2. We will never fully understand each other. That too is OK.

3. If we feel badly about someone not understanding, then it is our responsibility to change our feelings. This may prove to be a challenging therapeutic task.

4. When we are confronted calmly with our supposed lack of understanding, what is required of us is a willingness to listen.

5. What is also required is finding the courage and ability to talk calmly with those who don't seem to understand us, *provided they are important people to us.*

In summary, expecting or needing understanding from others is a trap that causes much unhappiness for those so ensnared. To disengage from this trap may prove difficult and time-consuming, but definitely worthwhile.

YOUR GROUP HAS THE SAME PROBLEMS AS ACME INC.

This section applies to all groups, not just corporations. It applies to couples, families, social groups, service groups, therapy groups, as well as corporations.

Consider a mythical company, Acme Inc., with its better mousetrap designed by Acme's founder, Ms. Acme, several years ago. At first there were five employees, all trying their best in somewhat flexible roles to make a go of the new venture. Over time these roles tended to harden into concrete, thus solidifying the hierarchy. After a few years, all became aware of the possibility of selling two different types of mousetraps rather than one. Mabel, who handled orders by hand, did not like that idea because it would have created extra work for her. If the group is still new enough so that roles are not strongly fixed, then Ms. Acme or Mr. MBA may accurately see the need for computers and be able to take appropriate action. If roles have become fixed, however, there will be a strong tendency to "support" Mabel and make the decision that "it is no doubt better to stick with one mousetrap- after all it is a winner." This is *Going-Along-Disease*, discussed later in this chapter. It is not just Mabel, for members of all groups have the tendency to define their own procedures and responsibilities as the Gospel According to Our Group. Because of changes over time, however, the old policies and procedures are no longer as effective or competitive as they once were.

Because of this Gospel, any other groups or individuals who disagree with the Gospel are *judged* as wrong or bad, divisive, evil, etc. Even if our group Gospel is badly out of date, it will be protected and its detractors will be *blamed* (Stage II). This I call *Blaming-Others-Disease*, to be discussed in more detail later. Mr. Sales, who learned his sales techniques on used-car-lots, makes his rounds of stores and has not significantly changed his pitch over the years. He doesn't realize that the hard-driving techniques that initially won him their accounts are becoming detrimental to his success at maintaining sales. He continues them because they have become his Gospel. Mr. Sales blames the customer for not buying, and for being the cause of his poor sales record.

The opinion of other group members becomes Public Opinion and part of the group Gospel that is rigidly held in great reverence. Because most of us prefer stability and routine, we tend to go along with "the way we did it last time," and this is rewarded with favorable Public Opinion. Mabel will often get her wish to "do it the way we did it last time."

Major structural changes, such as changing from a manufacturing company to a more service-oriented organization will often prove to be impossible. Such a direction, however necessary, will be resisted not only out of staff stuckness. It may be resisted too because that group of people at Acme Inc. may be incompetent to make such a change happen. *In truth, almost all groups are set up to be resistant to major change.*

A group will have strengths and weaknesses depending upon those making up the group. Particularly if the group becomes closed to outside information, group flaws over time will be neglected, denied, glossed over, repressed and "supported" by the phrase, "It worked OK for us that way last time." Without change in this rapidly changing world, our groups (yes, Acme Inc. and *all* our groups) become about as relevant as the National Association of Buggywhip Manufacturers.

GOING-ALONG DISEASE

One particularly destructive trait of groups is what I am calling "going-along disease." It is a learned tendency to go along with whatever is happening in our group, whether or not we agree. To voice our disagreement would probably cause us to be labeled as divisive and uncooperative. Therefore, it often takes great courage to speak one's truth when in a group. Furthermore, it goes against what most of us learned as children where adults made the rules. The failure to speak up, however, leads either to: (1)group stagnation - "let's do it the way we did it last time" or (2)group deification - "our group is better than any other." People who are noxious to outsiders often later in a group's life become spokespersons who serve to alienate the group from outsiders, an alienation for which those outside the group will no doubt be blamed.

*I am not an Athenian
or a Greek, but a
citizen of the world.*
Socrates c. 400 B.C.

BLAMING OTHERS DISEASE

The tendency for groups to blame others for their difficulties is so widespread that at times it seems almost universal. While we often do this as individuals, blaming others for our personal problems, it as members of groups that we excel in this accusatory trait. It is one of the major neurotic (i.e., skewed) reasons why we join groups. They often provide refuge for us with like-minded people who will agree with us that our problems are *out there* instead of within. If there any perceived truth in our blame of a particular target, then we are often quick to place *all* the blame on that target. This excuses us from looking at ourselves.* How convenient!

Verbal bashing is rarely seen as a trap. There is a sense of being on the side of justice, and the process of bashing seems to make one feel better (temporarily at least). Unfortunately, this process is no better than making oneself feel better by smoking, by drinking, or by another addictive behavior. Why? Essentially, bashing just releases steam without facing one's real issues beneath the anger. (A stage of blame is necessary, but is not effective when directed at people/ groups of today - see chapters 9 & 10.) In all likelihood, bashing will produce a painful backlash. Confirmed bashers will feel righteously indignant about the backlash and often trap themselves into more bashing. **VERBAL BASHING IS A TRAP!**

Finding Out About Our Own Groups Exercise

(1)Make a list of all the groups to which you belong. (2)For each of these groups, think of who is *excluded*. (3)Think of ways you can be *appreciative* of each of those who are excluded (this may be tough - these are often our most unpopular Earth School teachers)

EFFECTIVE ACTIVISM TODAY

It was refreshing recently to witness a newer highly-effective style of activism being used by women trying to change the system of breast cancer research. What was immediately evident was their lack of blaming and anger. There were determination, focus and clarity to find out just what the problems were.

Lo and behold, these women discovered that instead of the current research being a sexist problem, it was more a *group* problem. Breast cancer researchers and government officials had established their own hierarchies and kept researching virtually the same things over and over. (In mousetrap terms, they kept researching spring-loaded mousetraps without looking for any other ways of catching mice.) The activists were able to change this research focus in a matter of months of media attention. (Planning by those women no doubt took longer.) Many problems with governments, businesses and other groups today are just such hierarchical problems. They may have had historical roots in sexism, racism or anti-gay feeling; but today such hierarchical problems often topple without that much effort because society has changed. They topple more readily when approached with calmness and determination instead of anger and blame.

Unfortunately, there remains much old-style ineffective *blaming* activism. Activists (women, blacks, gays or whoever) are often among the first to be offended by others' lack of understanding, yet frequently they themselves show little understanding of the 80% of the population friendly to their causes. For that friendly 80% is typically alienated by activism that unexpectedly costs them money or time. Also, they are increasingly turned off by the bashing rhetoric. Activists who are locked into the *bashing of others** probably need to be reeducated or replaced by their parent organizations.

Newer activists often see things differently and promote debate within activist hierarchies. The result of such debates is often more effective activism, such as evidenced by the women who recently tackled where the research funds go in breast cancer research. Let us celebrate the new activists!**

THINK GLOBALLY, ACT LOCALLY

To change the world out there, we need first to change our own actions in our own groups. To effectively change our own groups we need to think more globally. How does my group appear to outsiders? (If your group regularly offends the 80% of white males friendly to your cause, is that productive for your group today?) As individuals our local actions need to include stopping our *going-along* with "the way we did it last time" and our blaming-of-others game. We need to voice our opinions to tone down the rabid radicals within our groups. This will not be easy. But it is worthwhile for two reasons: (1)our self-esteem will be heightened and (2)our group's effectiveness will be improved.

Sometimes our busyness with our special group(s) can obscure the truth that we <u>are</u> all citizens of the world.

---

*   See Appendix A

** Possible additions to your I-WANT-LIST (see Appendix C):
      I want to speak up in my _____ group.
      I want to appreciate those *outside* my _____ group.

The predicament of someone who tries to meet all of society's masculine-feminine standards.

Chapter 13
Women & Men

OUR MASCULINE-FEMININE MISCONCEPTIONS

Clearly women and men *are* different at genetic levels (such as X and Y chromosomes) and carry different sexual equipment. But beyond those obvious differences, I believe much of our societal thinking remains flawed concerning male-female and feminine-masculine characteristics. Sensitivity used to be considered feminine and competitiveness was considered masculine. Today some believe that we all have equal capacities for such traits as sensitivity and competitiveness. This newer belief also seems flawed and causes distress for many.

We would all be happier if we believed that all so-called masculine and feminine characteristics such as left/ right brain thinking, intuition, physical activities, vulnerability, competitiveness, anger, grief, nurturing abilities, etc. were possible characteristics for everyone. I would agree that anyone who *totally* denies any of these traits is not fulfilling his/ her potential (probably in response to early training and trauma). *That does not imply, however, in some hypothetical perfect society that women and men would display equal quantities or qualities of these characteristics.* Instead, there is much evidence to suggest that there are inherent tendencies caused by hormones and genes that promote or inhibit these qualities.

I WANT A CHEESE SANDWICH

So therefore I go to the kitchen. As a typical man I head straight for the supplies - bread, cheese, mayo, a knife and a plate. The state of the kitchen is not even in my consciousness - the dishes in the sink, the overflowing garbage pail, the toys on the floor, etc. Whatever lacks relevance in my mind to the cheese sandwich I will probably overlook.

As a typical woman I sometimes think that my spouse thinks exactly the way I do. "Of course he notices the dirty dishes, the overflowing garbage and the misplaced toys! He is just being difficult or he's trying to get back at me in some way by pretending not to notice. It seems I now have a choice either to do the chores myself or to confront him with his lack of sensitivity and caring, also his wrongness."

No matter which of these two likely choices she makes, the man in her life will probably consider her *illogical*. "Didn't she go out to the kitchen for a cheese sandwich and then for some weird illogical reason wind up chastising me (or doing the dishes)?" Instead of lacking logic, the woman has gone through an involved thinking process involving ideas, beliefs and decisions. A change in focus away from the cheese sandwich was the natural outgrowth of that process. She has been most logical. She just has not shared every step along the way with her spouse. (And make no mistake about it, he really does <u>not</u> want to hear all the steps in that process.)

The most important point with this cheese sandwich mini-saga is that men and women typically *think* very differently. (Do you agree?) While there are, of course, millions of exceptions, women tend toward internal debates, good/ bad thinking and sorting behavior. Men's thinking typically has few words (i.e., what <u>feels</u> right usually causes the next action). Neither the typical male nor the typical female thinking pattern is right or wrong. To try to change my spouse's basic thinking pattern is likely to be harmful to my relationship, for that shows a lack of love on my part for that person today. Some women today are trying to change men's basic thinking pattern and vice-versa. They won't succeed. These patterns are strongly evident even in the earliest years of life. Two-year-old girls are already verbally chattering away while two-year-old boys are more often just nonverbally pushing things around, uttering few words in the process. *Men and women typically do think differently and that is OK. Also - contrary to popular opinion, women are rarely illogical.* *

MEN DON'T LISTEN;
MEN DON'T COMMUNICATE

As described in the preceding section, the average male is far less verbal than the average female. Therefore, it will often be the case that he tunes out her words very quickly. How many women can truly accept that their man will *never* be willing or able to verbally communicate, either by talking or by listening, to women's standards?

If a woman could accept such a *never*, then she might galvanize herself to learn different methods that might lead to much increased effectiveness of communication. There *are* ways, but they will often not look like the typical communications among women. These ways involve increased *quality and effectiveness* of the communications attempted. Some suggestions follow that presume a mythical/ average couple who want better communication (Note-these suggestions do not depend upon their spouse's actions):

(1)She must reduce her quantity of words. After a certain length of time he will tune her out no matter what. He must be more truthful about when he starts tuning out and why.

(2)She must be careful about preciseness. An accusation that he never takes out the garbage when he knows he took it out once three months ago may lead to his rejecting everything she says. He must express how he is affected by such globalizing comments.

(3)In his seminars on relationships Gary Smalley describes a method he calls *word pictures.* This method involves communicating feelings by word pictures.

There are many books written about communication. Whatever your sex, read them if communication is a problem in your relationship(s). Almost all of us could learn to be more effective communicators with the people in our lives.

LEFT BRAIN - RIGHT BRAIN

There is such confusion about this matter! Let me simplify - the verbal, sorting, detail-oriented side of the brain is the left, whereas the spatial intuitive nonverbal side is the right. Who is more verbal, the average man or woman? By a wide margin, of course, the answer is the woman. She speaks twice as many words as the man and has done so even before the age of two. Boys and men are much more nonverbal, usually preferring physical spatial activities even as small toddlers. So the evidence is clear that women hang out more in their left brains, whereas men tend to hang out more in their right brains.

Am I saying that beer-guzzling/ TV-glued/ sex-driven man in your life is more intuitive than you, the average woman? Yes, for he senses a situation and takes action intuitively (though his responses may be very restricted). He does not go through a long internal verbal process in choosing his path - he reacts, knowing it is right for him to do so. Intuition is defined (*Oxford,* 1980, s.v. "intuition") as "the power of knowing or understanding something immediately without reason or being taught." He responds immediately with sexual feeling to sex objects (no planning or long decision making process for him in these matters). This is an immediate response to his feelings (i.e., right brain work). If you say something he doesn't want to hear, he will not respond verbally, but spatially as he moves to the TV to watch hockey reruns. He senses your words are wrong for him, and his intuitive response is to move away. As a woman, on the other hand, you may have long debates in your head before you come to make a decision or take some action. Such internal thinking and debating are left brain activities.

> **Note to Women.** Men are not generally as comfortable on the verbal side of their brains as you are. When you say to them "let's talk," you are asking them to join you in an activity in which most men feel somewhat inferior to you. As soon as possible, many men therefore will opt out of talking to return to their preferred nonverbal spatial activities.

There is major confusion between the words intuition and creativity. Intuitive people are not necessarily creative, some just keep duplicating old ruts without much conscious left brain thinking. Creative people, on the other hand, manage successfully (though perhaps only temporarily) in the intuitive right brain.

Major contributors to the confusion about left-right brain activity are feelings, which usually have been attributed to the right brain. It has been a recent societal value to consider right brain activities as more desirable. Yet some recent research suggests that happy feelings reside in the left brain and unhappy feelings in the right brain. Who wants to rush to be the right-brained person now?

Because men do seem to have more difficulty with feelings, it has been often believed that men must not be in the right half of the brain. On the contrary, they often compensate for their difficulties with certain feelings by feeling others. Typical compensations are: (1)they may feel sexual in all sorts of situations that are not particularly sexual, (2)they may just head for their TV addiction instead of hanging out with an uncomfortable feeling or (3)they may get angry in situations that might call for a different response. Men, when they repress their feelings, do not routinely move to the verbal left brain. They often stay in the right brain and compensate by feeling other feelings or by choosing some addictive behavior.

Thus, I make the following assertion that is contrary to much published information: *women are more left-brained, men are more right-brained* (perhaps 80-90% of men and women).*

Test Yourself for Left-Right Brain Tendencies. A one-question quiz (without scientific basis) may give you a good clue. The question is - "Assuming you hold up your share of the words, do you usually spend more than an hour each week on personal phone calls?" If you do, you have left-brain tendencies. If you don't, you have right-brain tendencies.

Of course, many situations are more complex or are exceptions: (1)many men and women don't fit the typical mold, (2)lefthanders often are the exception, (3)the average woman may have better access to both halves of the brain and (4)men often seem to shift from wholly left to wholly right and back rather than find a middle ground with ready access to both halves (as might the average woman). These more complex situations tend to confuse us.

Each of us would do well to examine our own favorite brain location. Historically, women and men have tended to cluster in occupations that fit the above described right-left brain tendencies. The choice of our jobs is vital to our happiness (see Chapter 14). Selections based upon some socially-correct view of today, instead of our own natural inclinations, could well produce much unhappiness in our lives. Non-traditional job opportunities are vital for that significant minority of both men and women whose natural gifts (and favored sides of the brain) are non-traditional. Because men and women have different preferred sides of the brain, it seems a faulty goal to have a 50-50 female-male balance as a societal goal in any occupation that is left-right brain oriented. (On the other hand, equal opportunity is desirable, as is equal pay for equal work.)

THE HOUSEWORK BATTLEFIELD

Men are often just trying to pacify women concerning housework. Women are usually the ones unhappy about the lack of housework help from their spouses. Many women fail to see that they have been overtrained and

_Life for Both Sexes Is
Arduous, Difficult,
a Perpetual Struggle. It
Calls for Gigantic Courage
and Strength._
Virginia Wolff

traumatized as young girls by their mothers. Therefore, they have all sorts of standards and *shoulds* which to their spouses are just simply absurd. (Leaving the microwave door open is <u>more</u> efficient. Leaving an often-used can opener on the counter is <u>more</u> efficient. Putting clothes in a drawer makes them <u>less</u> accessible. Dusting seems irrelevant. Why do the dishes before clean ones run out? Finally, doing it all so often seems ridiculous to many men.) Women often fail to assume responsibility for their unhappiness in this area, demanding that their spouses change. Instead, I suggest that women try using two of their strengths, planning and logic.

What planning and logic can accomplish is the training of men to notice a <u>few</u> things, those things that by joint agreement are to be the man's responsibility. Beyond those items that become the man's responsibility, women had best learn to expect and accept complete obliviousness. Otherwise, a woman may burden her relationship with added strain because of her unhappy judgments about what her man should be doing about housework.

Yes, the average man needs to do more housework, but not to the average woman's standards.*

FRIENDS BETTER KNOW THEIR ROLES

What men expect from their male friends is usually very different from what women expect from their female friends. Yet, both sexes' expectations lead to difficulties with friends.

For example, consider a situation where a couple, John and Mary, have an hour-long argument over their child's schooling. Afterwards, Mary talks to her female friend for a long time about the argument: what he said, what she said, what she felt, how inconsiderate he was, a long drawn-out almost blow-by-blow description of what happened together with her feelings about the entire situation. Mary's friend is always supportive: asking what he or she said next, agreeing with Mary about how inconsiderate John was, saying how right Mary was to feel the way she did, etc.

John, on the other hand, probably won't mention the argument at all to his male friend. If he does, it will be a very brief comment such as "Mary and I had a fight last night about Sonny's schooling." John's friend, if he ventures more than "Oh", may say something along the lines of, "Have you sent her flowers recently? Let's go play golf." John's friend does not want to hear all the details and would probably have preferred that John not raise the topic at all.

Yes, this is stereotypical behavior by both Mary and John (and their friends), but such behavior is widespread.

What neither the women nor the men in the above situation recognize is that both behavior patterns are faulty. Mary's pattern is faulty because: (1)She is always looking for support when she might often serve herself better by acting independently. (2)Frequently she is denying responsibility for her responses and digging herself a deeper rut by not looking for ways she might change. John's pattern is faulty because: (1)he is too often trying to make-it-on-his-own and (2)he avoids any leftover feelings by not talking with anyone, thereby not changing any rut he may be in. (If they fail to continue talking with each other about the topic, both Mary and John are displaying faulty communication patterns.)

Women like Mary will get most offended if their friend starts to ask questions along the lines of, "What might you do differently next time?" or "How might you respond differently next time?" John will tend to avoid the male friend who really tries to be supportive and elicit what really was going on inside John during his fight with Mary. Yet these changed responses from their friends could be useful in eliciting happier change for both John and Mary.

Do you have the courage to look for a friend who could be there for you in much deeper ways, rather than be unquestioningly supportive (Mary's friend) or be in total avoidance (John's friend)?

SUPPORT MAY BE DANGEROUS TO RELATIONSHIPS

When I ask people whether they know of any disadvantages to being supportive, they often reply "no." Yet there are two crucial not-so-obvious disadvantages which accrue from being too supportive in relationships.

One problem develops over time. To remain supportive, silence rather than open expression of differences often becomes the preferred choice. Keeping silent for too long is injurious to one's mental health, for psychosomatic complaints and other psychological symptoms are frequently caused by choices (conscious or unconscious) to remain silent. Over time these choices to remain silent develop into a "laundry list" of unspoken differences. If now spoken, then the relationship might well be broken under the weight of all the differences.

Therefore, the choice often becomes either to keep on being silent or to just break off the relationship.

The silent person is not the only one who suffers. The relationship does too. There is a basic trust issue, which those who overvalue support tend to overlook. Whoever is being supportive is often hiding a wealth of opinions and ideas from the person being "supported". Truths are being hidden "out of consideration for" the person being so "supported". Many "support" their spouses/ bosses in this fashion and spill their true opinions and ideas to others. Often these are the same people who complain that their spouses don't trust them. Of course not. Trust involves openness and honesty, not hidden ideas and opinions and most especially, not sharing hidden ideas and opinions with friends instead of spouses. Because of this trust problem, being too supportive will often doom a relationship, which is a fact not often realized by those overvaluing supportive behavior. (I am not advocating brutal honesty 100% of the time, but I *am* advocating more honesty by many who overvalue support.)

There is a real difference between "support" and genuine acceptance. "Support" typically hides criticism, lack of acceptance, lack of forgiveness and lack of love. Genuine acceptance means that the other's foibles and failures are OK (*one's opinions have usually already been shared with that partner and need no further expression to anyone*).*

THE INSENSITIVITY OF MEN

Sensitivity is a popular word these days, spoken often by politically-correct groups. The usual implication is that males don't have it, and said lack is one of the major causes of society's ills. There is some truth in the perceived lack of male sensitivity. Men, more often than women, have difficulty with loving feelings, being vulnerable, and with grieving. These are vital human qualities that men have often lost and that may take much time and therapy to regain. Often men are not even aware that they are hurting. The denial of pain and hurt is widespread, particularly among men. For them it is often safer to stick with the anger than to face any of the fear and hurt beneath the rage.* It is often an important part of men's personal growth to become aware of and sensitive to discomfort, fear and hurt.

Men's processes of regaining valuable sensitivity are happening, though not always in obvious ways. The changes are often happening right on our TV screens. Who among us did not get some sex therapy during the

The Great Question...
Which I Have Not Been Able
To Answer, Despite My Thirty
Years of Research Into
the Feminine Soul, is
"What Does a Woman Want?"

Sigmund Freud

Clarence Thomas-Anita Hill controversy? Everyone was talking about it, what was OK, what was not OK, what men thought, what women thought - sex therapy for the entire culture. How many millions of men witnessed the retirement ceremony of basketball superstar Magic Johnson and his ability to say "I love you" to teammates and family? What about his ability to just let the tears flow down his cheeks? Many men viewing this were moved to look at themselves and talk among themselves, which is an essential step in the recovery of lost vulnerable qualities.

Standards for total sensitivity are held to be "right and proper" by some of us, yet is this not impossible? How could we ever be totally sensitive to groups of which we are not a part? We are all insensitive in some degree, because your experience is not mine, nor mine yours. This often has nothing to do with prejudice, racism, sexism or homophobia. Our differences in life experience will cause others' reasoning, ideas, and problems (particularly if their groups have been distant from my experience) to be less real and less understood by me. Instead of demanding total sensitivity, the key here is to not respond unhappily when we are misunderstood (see previous chapter).

THE SAGA OF JOHN DOE (white male, average guy)

Twenty-five years ago, John (a white male) started getting accused by groups of women, blacks and gays of being sexist, racist and homophobic. John was genuinely surprised at the attacks. Over time he looked at the complaints, agreed with many of them, changed many of his ideas about himself and about those groups, agreed to laws protecting the rights of these groups, and even agreed that he probably needed to become more sensitive, more caring and more vulnerable.

Now, 25 years later, John is more sensitive, more caring and more vulnerable (though not to Jane's standards). Yet he still hears the same accusations, many of which he now finds not reflective of what he knows about himself. He *knows* that he no longer feels superior to women or blacks (the essential definition of sexism/ racism) and he *knows* that other sexual orientations are not fearful to him anymore. He finds that if he voices disagreement with anything these accusing groups might say, he is again instantaneously labeled sexist, racist or homophobic. And he finds more and more to disagree with in the rhetoric being spouted by the more militant members of such groups. John is being expected to understand others perfectly. If he doesn't, he is on the receiving end of hate, vituperation and blame. John's real choice today about such unreasonable demands is whether to join the backlash or to remain silent.

John is not perfect, but he is definitely growing psychologically in many areas. Those who believe that John is still like his old buddy Archie Bunker fail to see how much John has changed over the years. Men with the old views are definitely in the minority today, which ought to be cause for celebration by women, blacks and those of alternate sexual persuasions. John's growth has not been matched by *some* of his accusers, however, who seem locked in a pattern of blaming and judging others. Such judgments always create unhappiness for those making the judgments. (You might choose to review Chapter 8 for more about judgments.)

For those attempting to change John today, the old blame technique is rapidly losing effectiveness (it will probably never work for the remaining small minority of Archie Bunkers). For outside groups to affect John today will require that such groups be willing to shoulder their responsibilities for changing themselves by ridding themselves of their bashing rhetoric and their flawed thinking.

THE INSENSITIVITY OF WOMEN

If women were really sensitive to their men, they would realize that *as it is often currently promoted*, sensitivity is NOT wanted by many males."Why should I be sensitive? Who wants to feel hurt? OK, she says that I'm insensitive, I'll see what I can do to play along and put up a good show of sensitivity." Instead, it would more effective to promote that a man needs to regain his sensitivity (1)to feel complete, (2)to get out of anger traps, (3)to feel good, (4)to avoid emotional crippling, (5)to improve his relationship with a woman, (6)to rid himself of addictions or (7)to reduce stress.

Women also tend to be insensitive to men in areas where women apparently have received significant trauma. In our society this translates to sexuality (see Chapter 15), competitiveness (see Chapter 14) and anger (see Chapter 9).* In these three areas, some women often show a complete lack of sensitivity to men's issues. They also tend to judge harshly the differences between the sexes, judgments which often, I believe, blame the wrong sex for the difficulties. Of course, men too frequently misjudge women's views in men's areas of significant trauma and diminished capabilities - sensitivity, caring, empathy and communication (see Chapter 9).

FEMINISTS ARE A DIVERSE GROUP

The emerging diversity within the feminist movement seems to me important for the mental health of our entire society. The thoughts and ideas now voiced by some spokeswomen seem much more valid to me (and to others) than what has been expressed in the past. Past feminist bashing of and nonstop anger at men has alienated most men and many women from those who have been voicing such angry ideas. Alienation does not lead to change; it leads to a backlash. A woman's ability to find a happier spiritual system (see Chapter 11) will provide her with much more happiness, self-esteem and contentment than will the conventional *fight* response advocated by many feminists. Such a fight response often leads to anger without end. Is that happy or healthy? Do you want that for yourself?

I think that Gloria Steinem in her *Revolution From Within* really hit the bull's-eye when she discussed the fact that men also suffer from lack of self-esteem. Low self-esteem is virtually a universal problem in this culture (in our problem areas, we *all* feel low self-esteem). It is a lack of self-esteem that propels a man to attempt to put down a woman or to be threatened by her as a boss. Men who feel good about themselves (i.e., have self-esteem) have no need to put down anyone. It is the perception of many women that men do have self-esteem. Instead, fragile bravado often accurately describes the actual situation, particularly in their relationships with women.

A few of the more controversial feminists in the early 1990s have voiced strong opinions concerning verbal harassment. They have said that there is no such thing as verbal harassment - that whatever words are voiced, we each have a choice to be the "victim" of such words or not. (For more, please see Chapter 8 under the heading, *Sticks and Stones*.) Such is a most politically-incorrect view. During the Hill-Thomas hearings, a female Member of Congress voiced the politically-correct view when she criticized a man for wanting the details of what had been said before he would accept a charge of harassment. The legislator's response was that if it felt like harassment, it was harassment. This criterion is popular with some, but seems to completely discount people's abilities to be in charge of their own emotional responses.

While there has been a skewed backlash against the women's movement, there has been a legitimate backlash as well, because of (1)bashing rhetoric, (2)inherent male-female differences and (3)feminist excesses. The rhetoric that blames only men and excuses women for the difficulties of women overlooks or totally excuses the roles our mothers (and other female figures such as teachers) played in our development. Such rhetoric often consigns its believers to perpetual trauma knots concerning their mothers. By the same logic that some feminists use to excuse their mothers from all blame, they could as easily use to excuse their fathers. (Didn't their fathers just learn what was taught them? How could a boy of three know that he was being messed up by the widespread training in chauvinism?) Of course, if all current blame were dropped, the feelings of the child within would remain. Those upsetting inner-child feelings are precisely what are being avoided by focusing solely on current-day blame of males.

The skewed backlash against women is composed of people with an inability to change significantly. When they reach their limits of change, they rebound (or backlash). The essence of the problem with men in this category is typically their problem with grief. They are unable to shed tears and therefore are unable to release their trauma knots. And they do have trauma knots such as "be strong, be a man, be strong for Mommy/ Daddy, big boys don't cry, women are weak to cry, physical strength is everything, size is related to the importance of the person." To permanently release many of these trauma knots, grief is needed (see Chapters 9 & 10). I believe that if the women's movement were to be forever vigilant and active trying to promote male tears, the neurotic backlash by men would dissipate. Similarly, the neurotic backlash by women seems to reflect inabilities in the area of anger and hatred (see Chapter 9), which contribute mightily to low self-esteem.

While the work of feminism is not complete, it is possible NOW to celebrate what has been accomplished.

FEMININE? MASCULINE?

We might all be happier if the words feminine and masculine were banned. Few, if any of us, fit *all* the traits evidenced by the majority of our own sex. (Many women are aggressive and active. Many men hang out in the "non-masculine" side of the brain. Most of us have non-traditional activities/ times in our lives.) We all have abilities for intuition, logic, vulnerability, feeling, assertiveness, softness, harshness, competition and nurturing. To label any of these traits as masculine or feminine just causes unhappiness in our society.**

*Let's celebrate the human
abilities we all have.*

* See Appendix A

**Possible additions to your I-WANT-LIST (see Appendix C):
      I want to communicate more effectively with women/ men.
      I want to develop better friendships.
      I want to celebrate diversity.

*This Is the True Joy in
Life, the Being Used for
a Purpose Recognized by
Yourself to Be a
Mighty One*

George Bernard Shaw

Chapter 14

Work

DOING WHAT YOU LOVE

The best prescription for improving your happiness might well be, "Do what you love." In other words, follow your work passion wherever it may lead.* While it may seem foolish to quit a current job because of potential loss of high pay, medical insurance or security, that is sometimes our best course. Marsha Sinetar wrote a valuable book about the topic, *Do What You Love, The Money Will Follow.* This book reassured its readers that the money would follow, but not necessarily immediately, if one made a work change in the direction of one's passion. Most of us take no action hoping that money and security will be there before we change vocations. Such is often not the case.

Doing what you love may seem impossible; but the stress, pain, injury and disease resulting from clinging to your old work may kill you. If nothing else, I suggest that you take a few small steps in the direction of your passion. If we believe this to be a safe universe (see Chapter 11), then such a leap into the job unknown becomes easier.

This author knows well the results of choosing occupations that pay poorly. Because of several career changes and other choices for lower-paying work, I have often been at the bottom of the financial heap as compared with peers. Despite the financial strains, I have no regrets about having followed my work passion wherever it led. Otherwise, I would no doubt be unhappily stuck in stress or addictive behavior.

THAT IMPOSSIBLE BOSS/ COMMITTEE

Is that boss really impossible, or is it you who need to change your responses? Are you and your friends playing out your childhood dramas by expecting too much from your boss? The neurotic issue most commonly dumped on bosses is that they don't care enough about us, the way Mommy and Daddy didn't care enough when we were young.

Do you regularly commiserate with fellow employees about your supervisor without accepting responsibility for the part you play? We sometimes use authority figures in our lives the way addicts use a fix, to avoid difficulties. We avoid our real issues by blaming the authorities (Stage II *blaming* - see Chapter 4). On the other hand, if we believed that our unconscious selves (or God, karma, higher power, etc.) brought such impossible people into our lives as growth opportunities, then we would demonstrate happier and healthier responses to our "impossible" boss.

Impossible bosses usually trigger our yet-uncompleted psychological work concerning early childhood authority figures. There has been a strong movement to avoid all authority in recent years - but that also avoids the authority traumas we suffered back them. It puts them on hold and often locks us into unsatisfying groups, jobs and committees. If we are unwilling to grow now, then we will probably just re-experience similar bosses in our next jobs.

JOB STRESS

Job stress is not an ideal name for the phenomenon. We get stressed everywhere. The key is *whether we can release the stress*, winding up in a state of ease. It has been popular to blame job stress on outside forces/ people, but if we cannot find ease, then we have a problem. Not everyone gets stuck-in-stress in dealing with my "impossible boss." Perhaps it is my growth opportunity to find a way not to get upset by that boss in the first place.

People get stuck in stress on the job for a variety of reasons:
(1)Many have problems with authority figures.
(2)The work is no longer interesting to them.
(3)They fear loss of a good health plan or high pay.
(4)They have to deal too closely with toxic situations (often requiring dishonesty or lack of integrity) or toxic people.

The key to handling all these stressors is *fear*. If fear responses can be changed, then the stress will ease and right action will be taken. If you are severely stressed in your job, please find yourself some therapy. Treatment for job stress is most often brief.

WOMEN'S & MEN'S WORK - WILL THEY EVER BE THE SAME?

Of course there should be equal pay for equal work. Of course any qualified person should be seriously considered for any position. Also, there are obviously many women who enjoy nonverbal physical jobs and many men who are most comfortable in verbally-oriented tasks. Society needs to accept and provide equal opportunities for such choices. But I think the statistics will be forever unequal, even if we come to a society with no sexism. For the evidence seems clear that men and women usually do emphasize different sides of the brain (see previous chapter). This automatically will lead the majority of men and women to different choices in work. Ideally, our work should be what interests us the most and also what we do best.

I doubt that equal male-female *representation* in any job category is either likely or desirable. In a previous chapter, I described how a typical girl is verbal and a typical boy is nonverbal (usually physically oriented). Does this continue to adulthood? Yes! What do we get but clusters of women in such verbal occupations as secretary, file clerk, and telephone operator? Meanwhile, men have clustered in nonverbal/ physical occupations such as tool operators, craftspeople and firefighters? Such clustering may have causes other than sexism.

One feminist response to such clustering would be to blame it on sexism and to also blame these paragraphs on male backlash. However, if the average woman naturally places more emphasis (than the average man does) on left brain activities such as sorting, details, and verbal activities, then any goal that tries to equalize male and female representation in the above job clusters is doomed. The average woman will be happier following her verbal left brain strengths and passions than following the more nonverbal physical route preferred by the average man.

The implications are many. A majority of women in a non-sexist society would probably *gravitate* toward being administrators, bankers, judges and accountants, also their traditional occupations such as secretaries, clerks and telephone operators. A majority of men in such a society would probably *gravitate* toward spatial and physical work as happens today. Many CEO jobs, which typically demand both styles of thinking, might well be filled by those with strong abilities on both sides of the brain.

Because men & women favor different sides of the brain , it is not desirable that equal numbers of each sex be in most job categories. Equal opportunity, on the other hand, is highly desirable.

DISCRIMINATION IN THE WORKPLACE

Recent statistics in some sections of the country have shown that for those under the age of thirty, equal pay for equal work has arrived in the workplace for women, Hispanics and African-Americans (it has been there for some time for Asian-Americans and gays). Great!

What often has been overlooked by those complaining about discrimination in the job market are the choices made by the complainants. Choices made by many of them (for occupations that either pay less or have very high unemployment rates) often perpetuate the disparity in income between them and white males. This is not necessarily *bad*, though it may seem so at first glance.

To follow are six of women's choices that contribute to their lower incomes:

(1)The frequent choice to drop out for a few years to raise children obviously lowers women's income statistics for those dropped-out years. But mothering experience also changes many women so that they often do not rejoin the climbing-the-ladder job track.

(2)The Type-A (workaholic) behavior often exhibited by executives who rise to the top is not chosen as often by women.

(3)Women often avoid physical jobs. For example, large companies such as the major airlines have made significant efforts without much success to attract women to good-paying jobs such as airline baggage handlers.

(4)Women have more often chosen advanced degrees that result in lower-paid people-helper jobs such as therapists than higher-paid business executives with MBAs.

(5)*Earning power* has been and is much more a cultural goal for men than for women (though this does seem to be changing).

(6)Entrepreneurial women in fields such as private-practice psychotherapist will, on the average, choose to charge less and thus make less than their male counterparts.*

African-Americans have often chosen occupations with dreadful unemployment rates such as musicians, artists, actors, basketball players (there are thousands attempting to fit in a few hundred slots), etc. This is rapidly changing now, for many new black lawyers, engineers and business majors are emerging from schools. Great! They will do far more to change the statistics than fifty years of government programs. (There is nothing wrong with picking a poor-paying occupation if that is your passion. But with that choice you may be contributing to the statistics you claim are caused by racists and sexists.)

THE GLASS CEILING

A favorite topic recently has been the unlikelihood of certain groups to attain high-level jobs. "Of course this is caused solely by discrimination" is the cry of many. Maybe not.

Historically there used to be the same type of glass ceiling for Catholics and Jews, but in those days no one called it a glass ceiling. Today, Catholics and Jews are well represented at top levels. But the process of reaching those top job levels is more than just overcoming discrimination. It also entails a wide range of past executive jobs. Until groups have that wide array of executive experience, the glass ceiling will be in evidence. There has been significant black executive experience in the military. One result was Colin Powell, our first black Chairman of the Joint Chiefs of Staff. If any group wants to break through the glass ceiling in significant ways, then they must first see the need for and then go after this wide array of executive experience. The glass ceiling is not caused solely by discrimination.*

Does your being unhappy about the current statistics (which support the idea of the glass ceiling) help you or those statistics? Please read Chapter 8 for more about changing your unhappiness (and in the process becoming more effective in making the necessary societal changes).

COMPETITION: WHAT WE LEARNED

We usually forget what it was like to be four years old. We were inferior in everything. Mom and Dad always knew more than we did about whatever topic came up. Seemingly they could do everything that we couldn't. They seemed like the biggest, strongest, most powerful people in the whole wide world. We did feel inferior, but that is normal for four-year-olds and felt OK unless we were put down or rejected for being that way. However, as the years pass, the desire to be as powerful and clever as our parents typically becomes important to us.

One therapy session with a young boy stays in my memory. While he and I talked of various topics, we were busily competing in a ball-toss accuracy contest. He consistently was the better of the two competitors. As the session was ending, in a serious tone he stated that he had won the competition. I replied, also seriously, "Yes, you did". Truth. And an obvious chunk of increased self-esteem was written all over his face as he walked away. He had accomplished his unconscious mission for that session, an increase in self-esteem.

If at an early age we suffered some form of rejection of our emotional selves (i.e., trauma most of us suffered), then it is likely that we will want to continue competing forever unless the trauma knots we suffered can be untied. The traumatized child, dependent and feeling inferior, often thinks that everything will be OK once he is bigger, stronger or more clever. Because getting bigger, stronger or more clever does not routinely change the trauma knots involved, many adults keep competing and competing. Such competing provides only temporary relief, such as that obtained from men's obsession with sports and women's obsession with shopping. Both are competitive activities (though some women deny the competitive aspects of shopping) that temporarily chase the inferiority hobgoblin.

Schools today are frequently attempting to give grade-schoolers success and praise for being the best at whatever. The essential point is not so much the importance of the activity ("you are a great hall monitor" is fine) as the feeling of self-esteem that helps overcome the natural stage of inferiority in young children. These school efforts are important but will not be completely successful with children who feel seriously flawed because of past or ongoing trauma experienced at home.

COMPETITION: GOOD OR BAD?

It is popular in some circles these days to bash competition. I think such bashing reveals more about the basher than anyone else. As described above, we all go through a normal growing-up stage where some competition is essential for development of healthy self-esteem. But what about adult competition? I don't think it essential psychologically, but it often provides some spice to life without necessarily harming anyone (shopping and sports are probably the most common examples). Competition can provide some relief of tension for someone with old competition-trauma-knots. While such tension relief over time may result in someone becoming addicted to competition, in comparison with many addictions a competition addiction is *usually* rather benign.

In the workplace, competition has received some bad press in recent years. Greed and layoffs are the two most frequently touted sins of competition. These two sins, however, can always be minimized with new rules (if the appropriate governing bodies are willing to live up to this responsibility of making such new rules) such as increased taxes on the greedy and work replacement/ training/ length-of-workweek rules for employees. We are always in need of newer updated rules for competition because of this changing society. Where there is no competition, such as on the government payrolls, there is institutionalized inefficiency. Didn't the old Communist nations convince us of the futility of governments producing efficiently? Isn't our own government's bloat impressive?

One key is to create rules that require companies to manage their businesses in the best long-term interests of the country as a whole, instead of the short-term interests of their stockholders. In that regard, rules and laws would be beneficial which (1)taxed companies heavily whose executives earned more than 30 times what their lowest paid employees earned, and (2)prohibited the sale by executives of their personal holdings of company stock until two years after they stopped working at that company.

Competitive systems will never be perfect, but reasonable application of new laws will keep the worst elements of competition at bay while producing the maximum of goods and services for us all. The alternative of government control soon becomes insensitive to the pocketbooks of those being governed. The belief that competition is somehow evil, while only held by a minority, is often given significant play in the media. This hurts progress, in my opinion, toward shaping the newer rules needed. I think that a healthy attitude considers competition itself to be neutral,* but that *competition regularly will be in need of corrections* as things get unfair.**

If your legislators are unwilling to create desirable rules for competition, then vote them out; or create and circulate your own petition for everyone's vote.

JOB DO'S

1. Follow your work passion.

2. If stuck with stress associated with your job, use this stress as a spur to your own growth so that you can eliminate the stress.

3. Change your negative *feelings and ideas* about current job statistics, the glass ceiling, your impossible boss, competition, job loss, etc.

We often do not trust ourselves or our world enough to follow our inner guidance concerning work.

* See Appendix A

**Possible additions to your I-WANT-LIST (see Appendix C):
     I want to pursue my passion for the following type of work_____.
        I want to read *Do What You Love, The Money Will Follow.*
        I want to feel more comfortable with competition.

Rx
Sex = Wild & Serious?

Often the best choice is a middle ground. In this sex case, on the other hand, we all would be happier with both extremes. With our partner we need <u>first</u> to face the serious consequences of our sexual behavior and take appropriate action to avoid sexually transmitted diseases and unwanted babies. <u>Next</u>, we need to allow ourselves to be sexually wild women and wild men. Millions of us tell ourselves that we can't be wild **and** serious. Stereotypically, if men had to get serious at any time during sex, they used to claim that spontaneity was inhibited (or they lost erections which they feared meant perpetual impotence). Stereotypically, women used to claim that raucous sex was somehow not OK for them. Neither of these stereotypical claims permits our full sexual expression. If your behavior is still significantly under the influence of these stereotypes, I suggest that you read further about sexuality. We unnecessarily limit ourselves if we deny either aspect of our **wild & serious** sexuality.

Chapter 15

Sex

SEX (as defined and described by a man): fun, raucous, wild, lusty, playful, ecstatic, hot, sweaty, spontaneous, exquisite.

SEX (as defined and described by a woman): serious business.

Which of the above definitions of sex most fit you? While those two definitions are, of course, gross exaggerations, they contain significant truth, even today. Women have received more negative training about their sexuality than men. To have a primary belief that one's sexuality is serious first and pleasurable a distant second causes the loss of much pleasure in many sexual processes. That belief also leads to much putting down of men for their "frivolous" behavior, not just because of serious consequences that men might be overlooking but because "sex should be serious and you men don't treat it seriously enough." In other words, to be lusty, wild or playful is not OK. The sexual sphere is one in which many men and women tend to judge the opposite sex as not being OK. Most making such judgments would feel better and be happier if they adopted some of the opposite sex's ideas about sex.

The current emphasis on *wild women* seems exactly right to me. It reflects the increasing awareness among women that *they* can change themselves. Let's celebrate the growing number of women who have found that it is better to empower themselves by eliminating their own unhappiness than to remain unhappily dependent upon the adage "men should change." It is popular with some women to bash male sexuality, but such bashing often seems an attempt to obscure women's difficulties with the topic. Those women who bash men's sexuality often deny they have difficulties with their own wild sexual enjoyment. Compassion (for men and women) would be a happier state for such women and also more effective in eliciting changes in men. Let's celebrate some of the newer feminists who *are* expressing more compassion.

The failure of men to be serious about the consequences of their sexual behavior has been very harmful to our society. Men have abandoned millions of children and have helped cause the spread of sexually transmitted diseases. Those acting so irresponsibly are probably not reading this book. But I hope that their partners (who may be reading it) can start demanding both serious and wild behavior from such men. For partners sometimes can be the catalysts for change.

Suggestion: In your own life try to make sex both lusty and serious.

THE CAVIAR OF SEX (as defined by a woman): sex in a context of a loving long-term committed relationship.

THE CAVIAR OF SEX (as defined by a man): sex with a Hollywood sex symbol.

While many, perhaps most, men eventually do move toward the above woman's view about the ideal sexual experience, this move usually does not come from following a "should." Instead, they discover that sex in a loving relationship is more satisfying than a quickie with a new partner. They change their view out of experience. Unfortunately, many men never seem to grow up in this regard because of their fear of a deep lasting relationship.

It is also unfortunate that many women who believe that loving sex is the caviar of sex often put down other forms of sexual expression. For them, sex in a significant relationship becomes the only OK form of sexual expression. While significant relationships might be wonderful, they are not always available. Not everyone at all times has them. Yet our sexuality is ever present. Sometimes it leads women into totally inappropriate relationships just to satisfy (1)a sex urge or (2)a neurotic trap of "you should be in relationship."

A belief in the necessity for an open marriage is not popular. Yet the *freedom* to explore outside marriage does seem essential for *some,* whether or not they do roam. Those who react most negatively to infidelity seem often confronted with it. Earth School lessons (see Chapter 11) may be at work here, giving such people roaming partners. Thus, they have the opportunity to move beyond their fears and unhappy feelings about unfaithfulness. Another @#$%^& growth opportunity! Many were horrified by the O'Neills' book, *Open Marriage,* and badly misinterpreted its meaning. (An open marriage does not imply that sex with partners outside the relationship *will* take place, but that the freedom is given to one's partner to do so.) Despite its controversy, *Open Marriage* contains valuable information about marriage and ways to move beyond one's discomfort with a roaming partner. I recommend that you read it if infidelity and/or a roaming partner are part of your life.

WHAT ABOUT YOUR DREADFUL SEXUAL DREAM LAST NIGHT?

You desperately try to forget that dream with its unapproved contents. It revealed the possibility of your worst sexual fears: the "wrong" partner, the "wrong" sex act, nakedness, exposure, impotence, incest, pedophilia, homosexuality, sadism, masochism, lack of orgasm, bestiality or _____. (Fill the blank with that dreadful sexual terror lurking within you.) Because of that dream you have immediately leaped to the worst conclusion about yourself. What next?

First, acknowledge your dread, as it is a valid truth for you that you need to explore. It doesn't usually mean that you are heading toward that particular dreaded sexual behavior. Instead, it is often a wake-up call for you to do your own therapy (with or without a paid therapist). Some psychological causes of such fears/ dreams are:

(1)Our Puritan heritage affects us all. See next section.

(2)Our childhood traumas of being excluded and abandoned by parents/peers often make it not OK to be different sexually. If this is the sole cause of your dreadful dream, then moving beyond those childhood traumas (which can take time) will end that type of dream.

(3)Often the dream-people give us the clue about where we need to grow. If I dream incestuously about a parent, I may need to explore [a]my childhood traumas associated with getting physical affection from that parent, [b]my inability to have such fantasies when I was four years old, [c]my fears of sex with an adult of that parent's sex and [d]the abuse I suffered at the hands of that parent. If I dream of sex that is not with adults, then I need to explore possible fears within me of being an adult sexually. If I uncomfortably dream of sadism or masochism, where did I suffer pain, abuse or degradation in my past?

(4)Many sexual dreams today are triggered by the traumas resulting from our lack of childhood emotional love and physical affection. Much sexual behavior in waking life is also driven by these old traumas of lack of love and

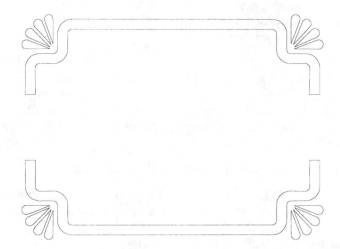

The above picture shows all those adults who have never had disquieting sexual ideas, fantasies or dreams.

affection. (But men on average would still have much more sexual interest than women because of testosterone even if all their neurotic sex drives could be eliminated.) Some homosexual dreams, for both heterosexuals and homosexuals, have their roots in fears of emotionally loving and being physically affectionate with members of one's own sex.

> **Tip.** A dreadful sexual dream is a wake-up call for you to look at yourself, not to leap to the worst possible conclusion about the dream's meaning. Disregarding the dream will often cause its return in a more dreadful form.

OVERCOMING OUR PURITAN HERITAGE

If you grew up in the USA, you have the heritage too, from TV and schools, no matter what your parenting figures taught.* Puritan training makes sexuality a minefield. "Sex is no good, should be hidden by clothes, should be used for making babies not pleasure, is wrong outside the sanctity of marriage, etc." While most of us do overcome most of this training as teenagers, vestiges frequently remain. I have two suggestions to overcome these vestiges:

(1)Self-talk that counters the training is useful. If I find myself talking or acting as if "sex is no good," then saying "my sexuality is OK" aloud five times will help counter the early training. Similarly, rephrasing of Puritan ideas to their opposite meaning and repeating them to myself often will be helpful. For example, "my body is OK just the way it is, sex is pleasurable and I enjoy it, I can enjoy sex without marriage or love, lust is great," etc.

(2)A frequent toddler trauma occurs when Mommy and Daddy enforce the rule against nakedness. What the toddler often learns from such a rule is that "My sexual parts are not OK," or "I am not OK." A particular fantasy can help significantly in healing this. Picture yourself as a toddler, the size of a small child, with Mommy (or other parenting figure) nearby. Or make Mommy huge if you have trouble making yourself smaller. Picture yourself naked, and say the words "I am OK, my body is OK, my sexual parts are OK, my body feels good" five times. This fantasy experience can result in significant healing of toddler trauma (and may also cause you to feel some childhood rage and grief).

Our Puritan heritage can be overcome, but to do so often takes time and significant effort.

SEX BY THE SCORECARD

Many were appalled by recent news about teen boys having a competition over how many different girls they had "scored" with. I believe 66 was the "winning" total. The public had many conflicting opinions such as: the parents were at fault, testosterone, boys will be boys, the girls brought it on, the devil's work, etc.

What blaming and finger pointing! As a society we are fragmented in the sexual area. We do not have a consensus about right/ wrong, natural/ unnatural, OK/ not-OK sexual behavior. Often in such cases it is fruitful to look at *what is needed*, rather than continue with the blaming and finger pointing. Those young men (who were in their late teens) needed to move beyond just the sex act and into emotionally loving relationships. That was their next stage of growth. Those teens were like many adult men who are afraid of emotional loving. (Fear of emotional loving also is prevalent among gay men who for long periods of time have multiple partners.)

Women often don't understand that many of today's teen girls do not feel degraded or put down by boys' scoring behavior. Instead of a lack of values, teen girls experience a more healthy exploration of sexuality than their mothers ever allowed themselves. The girls, sooner than the boys because of their societal training, will change their behavior to pursue the more satisfying combination of sex and relationship, .

When the message gets out enough to teens that such sexual behavior (scoring with many partners) is typically based upon fear of relationship, teens will reduce that behavior. Nevertheless, I believe that some "scoring goals" are likely to remain for those in their early teens. Full understanding of one's sexuality may require knowledge of one's sexuality both in and out of significant loving relationships. (Those who need to judge others in this sphere had best look at themselves.) One of the healthiest statements about sexuality I ever heard from anyone (a woman in this instance) was: "Over the years, casual sex became less and less interesting for me." She was not coming from a position of judgment or recrimination, but one of valued experience.

DO WE CHOOSE SEXUAL PREFERENCES?

There are widespread misconceptions among heterosexuals about those who are not 100% heterosexual. The question that each heterosexual needs to ask is, "Did I choose to be turned on by the opposite sex, or did it just happen?" For almost all of us, sexual arousal happens completely outside the control of our conscious minds.* Consciously we do not choose to be aroused by one sex or another.

Gay men and lesbians never <u>chose</u> to be aroused by members of the same sex. Few would <u>choose</u> to receive the ostracism and the hatred by others that so often come with not being heterosexual. Gay men and lesbians <u>do</u> choose to act or not act on that sexual arousal. Most gay men and lesbians go through a period where they try to become "normal" with attempts at (1)heterosexual acts (with more or less success) and/or (2)heterosexual relationships, often including marriage and children. Most <u>have</u> tried to become straight, and therefore they know by experience the absurdity of those who say that the goal ought to be to make them straight.

Sexual arousal *tends* to follow emotional loving feelings. Consider a stereotypical 24-year-old male who for many years had sexual fantasies and dreams of sex goddess bodies. He falls in love with a homely, overweight or flat-chested woman who then "magically" becomes highly attractive sexually to him.

> <u>**Tip for Men (Straight/ Gay/ In-Between).**</u> If you are looking for that great body first, you may never find your life-mate. If you love first, you will probably find the body you are with to be highly arousing.*

SEXUAL BOXES

Labeling one another as straight, gay, bisexual, etc. seems very important to many. Yet the distinctions are anything but clear-cut. We often use boxes to try to define others, but in truth our labeling says much about us. The labels themselves are often used (1)as negative judgments of others (judgments of others just bring the judge unhappiness- see Chapter 8), (2)as inclusion/ exclusion devices that promote alienation or (3)as fixed categories that do not allow for change. Many people don't fit readily into any box. For example, how do you label a person with mainly heterosexual dreams, fantasies and actions who has an occasional homosexual dream? There would be many different labels selected for this person depending upon who was doing the labeling.

I suggest that you give yourself a sexual label if you so choose, but that you allow others to be without a label unless they choose to label themselves.

What the labels don't allow for are the many who just don't fit the boxes, who seem over time to change boxes, or who may object to a particular label. (A criminal who enters prison with strictly heterosexual dreams and winds up leaving prison with mostly homosexual dreams is one example of a person temporarily changing boxes.)

Only a very small percentage of those attempting to change sexual boxes have achieved it by therapy or religious conversion. Many claimed "successes" are in doubt. If it is part of a person's lifeplan to explore alternate sexual behavior (part of the teachings of some spiritual systems) or if a person's genes cause homosexuality (a possibility), then any conversion treatment for such a person will fail. What those who use the term "pervert" (and its synonyms) imply is that alternate orientations are wrong. If homosexual behavior is so dreadfully wrong, why does it exist so prevalently in *natural* wildlife populations?

TREATMENT OF GAY MEN, LESBIANS AND BISEXUALS

Not too many years ago the American Psychiatric Association discarded the idea that homosexuality was a psychological disturbance. There are very few licensed therapists who have claimed any success in converting people with homosexual tendencies to the 100% heterosexual path. For most gay men, lesbians and bisexuals the possibility of such a change is most unlikely, nor wanted.

With gay men, lesbians, bisexuals and all others of alternate sexual orientations, therapy often focuses (particularly in the beginning) on becoming comfortable with the way they are sexually right now. This includes: [a] accepting themselves, [b] discovering how and when to tell others about themselves and [c] dealing with others' rejection.

Common therapy issues that are not sexual-orientation-specific (being sexual at all, anger, grief, self-esteem, addictions, relationships, etc.) often are the most important therapy issues. Treatment for these is much the same as it is for heterosexuals.

PORNOGRAPHY

Some societal groups keep on hoping that something dreadful will be proven about pornography so that it can be banished. To their discomfort nothing dreadful has been found.* These groups would do well to examine themselves, for discomfort about an issue like pornography always speaks worlds about those so discomfited.

The religious groups with strong opposition to pornography usually teach much repression of sexuality to their members. The Puritan ethic was mentioned earlier, and the Catholic influence will be discussed later in this chapter. In these groups, full expression of one's sexuality is not OK, and approved sexuality is narrowly defined within strict limits. Such groups often have no idea how destructive they are psychologically to their members who have different sexual orientations.

Most who believe that pornography degrades women are typically trapped by one of the following unhappy beliefs: (1)that one person can actually degrade another (see Chapter 9 for more about degrading), (2)that many aspects of sex between consenting adults are still not OK or (3)the only OK sex is in a long-term committed relationship. To change these ideas probably will require elimination of some beliefs learned in early childhood. The women involved in pornography may be degraded to some, but not necessarily in their own eyes. Many female porno stars treat it like a job.

Because so many pornographic scenes are chauvinistic, some believe that pornography must be correlated with increased abuse or maltreatment of women by the men who enjoy the pornography. This has not proven true. Most men's fantasies when they look at porn have not been shown to involve power or domination over the porn star or other women. Therefore, why would one expect a correlation between porn and violence toward women? Pornography has been a favorite area for some women to blame men, saying men don't respect women's sensitivity and hurt feelings about pornography. Such women are not even to the stage of understanding that their upset responses of hurt feelings and bruised sensitivities regarding pornography are *their* problems.

Yes, many men do search out porn for immature or fear-of-relationship reasons, but that does not mean that women need to continue feeling upset about such men. For there will always be many immature and relationship-fearing men. It has become popular for some women to make a blanket judgment of porn as "immaturity." They would understand far better if they talked with their sisters who have for medical reasons received testosterone shots. The

*Coition is a slight
attack of apoplexy.*

*Democritus of Abdera
c.460-c.370 B.C.*

hormone testosterone drives a person to much increased levels of (1)sexual interest, (2)erotic fantasies, and (3)sexual activity. Searching out pornography to discharge these increased sexual levels of interest seems to make sense for many.

If pornography bothers you, I suggest looking within at your own discomfort to see how you could change your unhappiness. There has always been (remember Pompeii?) and will always be pornography at some level or another out there. Do you wish to remain unhappy about it forever?

SEX & THE CATHOLIC CHURCH

Catholic clients often have sexual difficulties that are largely caused by the current teachings of the church. Hope seems to spring eternal in them that the church will somehow eventually make sense in sexual matters. However, that seems unlikely, given the fact that a major goal of those making the church rules is celibacy. Why would anyone expect sexual sanity from those who were pursuing (or cheating on) a goal of celibacy? Denying oneself such an important part of human functioning, one's sexuality, leads to much compensatory behavior (i.e., "saving" others, judging others, trying to feel good by doing good, alcoholism, etc.).

The desire to increase church membership also currently leads to condemnation of birth control. The church needs to get the message that no-birth-control just equals poverty. Instead, the church often blames the industrialized nations for not giving much of their wealth to the poorer nations. This blame helps the church remain in Stage I *denial* of any responsibility on the church's part for keeping poor nations poor.

To agree completely with the Catholic church in sexual matters just seems to lead to personal unhappiness. Therefore, most of my clients choose to disagree with the church's sexual promulgations while retaining their faith. They come to believe that (1)the church is peopled by fallible human beings and that (2)instead of swallowing some rather crazy sexual stuff, they have a personal responsibility to evaluate what those fallible humans in the church hierarchy might be saying.

RAPE

Differences in the definition of "sexual experience" have led in recent times to significant miscommunication about rape. It has become common to say that rape is not a sexual experience. Such a statement makes sense to most women, who identify with the helplessness facing such an inhuman power trip and with the pain of being so tortured. Typically, there is not one ounce of sexual pleasure. It feels like torture and is torture. The experience does not feel sexual. On the other hand, many men disbelieve the words, "rape is not a sexual experience." Their gut reaction is, "of course it is a sexual experience!" If one defines "sexual experience" as an experience involving the genitalia, their reaction is valid. Obviously, "sexual experience" is being defined differently.

A current question asked by some men reveals that they don't understand some current feminist thinking. The question is, "How can there be no distinctions between rape, date-rape and husband rape?" Fortunately, many women are now speaking out about the obvious distinctions.

It has become virtually impossible to voice any differing ideas about this emotionally volatile subject (rape) without being labeled as insensitive or worse. There are differing opinions out there, but as in the case of the pro-life/pro-choice clash, genuine discussion and acceptance of differences (which might lead to positive joint action) seems to be prevented by the emotional volatility.

SEX THERAPY

If you have the impulse to search out sex therapy for a sexual problem, do so. However, there are two elements of most such therapies that you may do yourself which may prove helpful:

(1)Education about body sexual parts may be accomplished by reading and/or by exploration with a willing partner.

(2)An early feature of sex therapy is often the touching and massaging of one's partner. At first sexual parts are avoided and then approached days later only if the massage goes well.

Often specific books on sexuality will be helpful. For men or women, I suggest *New Male Sexuality* by Bernie Zilbergeld and *For Yourself: The Fulfillment of Female Sexuality* by Lonnie Barbach.

A Tip for Men Making Love to Women

The old talk of a vaginal orgasm is considered bunk by many experts today. You men reading this will understand what many women want most, if you understand that the woman's vagina is like your testicles, enjoyable and important sexually. But without significant stimulation of the clitoris (analogous to your penis) orgasm and maximum sexual pleasure are not likely.

SEX THERAPY WE ALL RECEIVED

All of us received a major dose of sex therapy during the Clarence Thomas - Anita Hill controversy. Most everyone was talking about what was OK or not OK. Who was telling sexual lies? Then along came the Bobbitts, whose actions provided most of us with even more sexual lessons.

How best for a woman to respond to a situation such as described by Anita Hill? To say nothing to the man is the response that she said she chose for many years. That response fits many women's training, but it is an unhappy choice that is rarely useful today. She was not wrong. (Reminder- right/ wrong judgments of others just create unhappiness for oneself- see Chapter 8.) She chose the best response she could then. But would she suggest the same response for herself or others in the future? There are several responses that a woman could use effectively in such situations. (Obviously, there are some men with whom nothing will work.)

If the man is a supervisor, her response had best avoid judgments of him. Her response (a few days later is OK) needs to be verbal and delivered with eye contact. I suggest a response such as: "Mr. Smith, I am not interested in either a dating or a sexual relationship with you." (If he persists with "why," she can say, "I don't want that." If he persists, she can shift the conversation with, "Is there anything else concerning <u>work</u> that you wanted to talk with me about right now?")

If the man is neither her supervisor nor in a position of power over her, then the woman has the chance to be more open with her opinions. Again I recommend leaving out angry judgments, but a message such as the following would often work if delivered calmly and coolly: "I had no idea you were so sexually immature." A man receiving that message as he strutted his supposed sexual prowess and superior sexual equipment would most likely find a way to shut up fast.

Tip for Men Who Want More Sex. Many men are ignorant about how their sexual words affect women. Men who want more sex had best be students of how the women in their lives respond to both sexual and non-sexual words. Don't you men want more sex?

WOMEN AND MEN WILL NEVER BE THE SAME SEXUALLY

In recent years it has become popular to believe that if only those of the opposite sex would get rid of their hangups, they would act sexually like me. Wrong. While men and women are often the same, obviously it is in the sexual area of existence that we are often most different from each other.

(1)Different hormones coursing through our veins usually make men more interested in sex all the time and women *potentially* more emotionally volatile during PMS-time.

(2) The tendency for women and men to favor different sides of the brain causes (on the average) more female *talking* interest and more male *sexual* interest.

(3) Our bodies are different and do respond somewhat differently during sex.

It is our choice, to celebrate our sexual differences or to remain unhappy complainers about the opposite sex.**

Our society <u>has</u> come a long way
sexually in the past 30 years.
It's time to celebrate our
society's gains in sexual acceptance
of ourselves and others.

* See Appendix A

**Possible additions to your I-WANT-LIST (see Appendix C):
      I want to accept the following aspect(s) of my sexuality_____.
      I want to be more accepting of others' sexual orientations.

Families in therapy together? Yes,
often the most effective
treatment for some or
all members is family therapy.

Chapter 16

Families

ARE 97% OF FAMILIES NEUROTIC?

(In This Book: Neurotic = Skewed = Mild-to-Moderate Dysfunction)*

In an earlier chapter I baldly said that 97% of us grew up in dysfunctional families. That 97% statistic has circulated widely in recent years, although its accuracy has not been free of controversy. Given our skewed society, the truth is that all of us learned neurotic ways in our growing-up years: skewed thinking, skewed communication patterns, skewed emotional responses and skewed ways of treating our bodies. We learned dysfunction and became more or less dysfunctional depending upon how dysfunctional our role models and parenting figures were.

For most of us, our parenting figures were our most important teachers of dysfunction. They traumatized us with their abusive actions. They also gave us trauma knots with their demands, both subtle and overt, that we learn to stuff our feelings such as anger, tears, love and sexuality. Their demands upon us to remain silent, to not talk back, to take care of their feelings, to act strong when we felt weak, etc., increased our dysfunction. Their oft-repeated failures to meet our needs for love and affection skewed us immensely, as did their continued lack of respect for our individuality. The felt lack of caring from them traumatized us, whether it was caused by their addictions, by the dreadful parenting skills they acquired from our grandparents or by their adherence to "correct" child-rearing manuals of the times.

There are adults who honestly believe that their parents traumatized them not one bit. They claim most happy childhoods. In most of these cases denial is present. Their current claim of childhood perfection is contradicted by their addictive behavior such as smoking or drinking, their excess weight, or their unhappy relationships. Until such adults really look at what happened back then, it has been my experience that they continue a downward life course in terms of happiness. Potentially some are perhaps the healthiest among us, for their childhoods were generally good. Others claiming childhood perfection, of course, are in complete denial about a truly horrendous childhood, and they need their denial to protect themselves.

As I write this in the mid-1990s, there are many parents who have left most of the neurotic parenting behind. They accept the feelings of their small children, even hatred for girls and tears for boys. Instead of finding that their children are spoiled if their needs for affection are met, it seems the children are satisfied with *enough*. They don't become insatiable as do many adults, who are neurotically trying to make up for childhood lack of love. (Only by resolving that old trauma knot of kid-neediness will today's insatiable adults likely change their current never-ending neediness.)

If societal parenting is getting better, then why the increased violence among children? The reason is that parents have thrown out an important baby with the old neurotic parenting bathwater. The discarded baby is authoritarian messages, which will be discussed later in this chapter. *Authoritarian messages are crucial if we are to change our society's violent trends.** The media unknowingly support these violent trends with constant faultfinding of authority figures.

TRAUMATIZING CHILDREN - 97% OF THEM?

If you are a parent reading this and feeling guilty about your past or present parenting, please consider the possibility of being guilt-free (see chapter 9). You did the best you knew how at the time, but you may now want to rid yourself of guilt by developing a new spiritual system (Earth School compatible) as described in Chapter 11. It is your growth opportunity *now* to find a way to move beyond the guilt.

Most trauma inflicted upon children is not the obvious abusive kind in which the child gets beaten or molested, or hears "you are dumb" or "you are stupid." Instead, most trauma is less obvious. Its craftiness does not mean that it is not important! In fact, it causes most of our unhappiness, our hangups, our symptoms and our problems. There are four particularly damaging parental strategies that regularly and consistently create less-obvious trauma in our children. Two of these (those associated with sex and anger) tend to be inflicted more often on girls. The other two (those associated with sadness and sensitivity) tend to be inflicted more often on boys. The trauma message received (though not necessarily consciously) by the children is: "my anger, sexuality, sadness or sensitivity is not OK." The most common response of children so traumatized is to deny these aspects of themselves. This denial usually propels them *into a search for others' approval* (discussed later). If these four areas of trauma were even partially eliminated, our society would be incredibly and wonderfully different!

Today, many parents are doing OK with the above issues of sex, anger, sadness and sensitivity but fail to see the necessity for some authority. Children receiving this type of parenting (parenting without authority) are often either fearful or narcissistic (i.e., insensitive to others). Later as adults, they often: (1)blame others, (2)believe in conspiracy theories, (3)fear, hate or look down their noses at all signs of authority, or (4)"do their own thing" without awareness of how they affect others. As adults they also will be more insecure and more violent than those who have taken in authoritarian messages.

Let me give an example of why I think this new-style parenting cannot succeed with a significant percentage of children (30%, 60%?). Consider Bobby who just yanked his sister's hair. "We don't do that, Bobby. That is not nice, Bobby. Be kind, Bobby. Consider how she feels, Bobby." What Bobby learns from these parenting messages is that Mommy and Daddy will stop him if they are present. But he does not necessarily learn (**actually take in**) that his behavior is not OK and that morally it is wrong to pull hair. Further, what he may learn from that parenting style is that it is OK to do that, provided he doesn't get caught. (This skewed learning happens often today, because many parents are obviously disobeying laws of all sorts [55mph, inflating deductions or "forgetting" income on income tax returns, "enhancements" on resumes and credit applications, cheating the phone company or the grocery store, etc.]) The parents rationalize their actions without considering what their children are learning. Many children, like Bobby, are not capable of empathy for others, so the suggestion that they consider the feelings of others is lost upon them. Thus, a parenting style that lacks authoritarian messages is harmful to Bobby.

ARE WE REALLY HUMANE?

Most of us consider ourselves and our own groups to be humane and to evidence the highest qualities of humanity. Is this really so? A shocking psychology experiment casts serious doubts. Take average citizens and ask

<u>Authority Can Be Good?</u>

*Today many misguided
parents are teaching their children
that <u>all</u> authority is bad,
not just that bad authority is bad.*

them to "teach" one of their fellow citizens *nonsense* words in a psychology experiment. Then give them directions to electrically shock the "learner" (who is out of sight and in truth an actor-accomplice of the experimenter who never gets shocked) whenever the "learner" makes a mistake. The experimenter, dressed in a white lab coat, encourages the "teacher" to keep increasing the amount of electric shock to "teach them better." The actor-accomplice, out of sight but wired for sound, starts responding to the pretend electric shocks with small yelps, soon gives out cries of severe pain and when the most severe shock is supposedly given, is silent. Most "teachers" evidenced significant distress during the experiment. Nevertheless, *a majority of them followed the directions of the man in the lab coat to the very end, believing they were giving out severe electric shocks for failure to learn nonsense words.* These "teachers" were average citizens, not criminals, not severely emotionally disturbed.

Scary? Yes. Enlightening too, for the real lesson here is how out-of-touch with our humanity most of us can be without knowing it. Most of us can be vicious and cruel.

Treatment for loss or lack of humanity doesn't necessarily make it happen. There have been thousands of adopting parents who have discovered that "love does not conquer all." False caring, unfelt empathy and phony sympathy abound among cruel children and career criminals, for they try to please parents and parole boards with their professed humanity. The attempt to make these groups become humane is often the goal of jails, punishments, parenting and therapy. Such attempts are often failures. These failures can point us in the direction of more effective approaches, approaches which are *necessary* for many children (30%, 60%?).

EFFECTIVE PARENTING

Fifty years ago there was a widespread belief that sparing the discipline rod would spoil the child. In this flight from the discipline rod, something valuable that customarily went with the rod has often been lost - *verbal parental directives about behavior.* I am not suggesting bringing back corporal punishment as a routine measure. What I am suggesting is bringing back the *effective* verbal messages that parents often used in the past. Deliver these demanding messages authoritatively with direct eye contact, and in a tone that "accepts no nonsense." "You are not to steal! It is wrong to hit your sister! You are not to do that! You are not to pull the wings off butterflies!" Many (perhaps most) children seem to need such messages, though for some children they are unnecessary.

These messages are not traumatic. They _are_ authoritarian, and that has become a no-no for some of today's parents. Too bad. The children of these parents will have a much tougher time than those who do receive appropriate authoritarian messages. Young children thrive on right/ wrong, and good/ bad messages from parents - for several years that is their correct stage in moral development. Without such parental messages, they will tend to pick up morals anyway, from TV and friends. In this author's opinion, this is one significant cause of societal violence today: when parents aren't giving enough authoritarian messages, kids adopt TV values.

Will changing TV reduce societal violence? If my contention is correct that kids often adopt TV values, then TV could well add authoritarian instruction to its kid fare. Television _is_ a parent for many children today. I don't believe it is the TV violence level that is a major cause of our increased violence in society, for the Japanese (with many authoritarian parenting messages) have more TV violence and much less societal violence. Perhaps after three TV assaults of a cartoon-person, new laws could require that a real-looking parenting figure come on the screen for just a few seconds saying seriously, "it is _wrong_ to hit other people." (Then similar messages about stealing, killing, etc. could be aired.) Voice these messages in a neither sweet nor gentle tone, but in an authoritarian tone talking directly to the camera.

The most abusive messages are given by parents who say, "you are bad," "you are stupid," or "you will wind up in jail." These and other similar messages are taken in by a child and _often accepted as truth_ if said by a parent. Later, of course, the child receiving such early verbal abuse _will_ be a school dropout or in trouble with the law because of violence. (If you as a parent give out even <u>one</u> of these messages, you need to talk with that child about how you were wrong to do so and why you do <u>not</u> think that way about that child.)

OUR CURRENT FAMILIES
BRING OUT OUR SKEWNESS

The mates we select, the children we raise and the parents who raised us are the ones who trigger our buttons most effectively. We are at our most skewed around these people: quick to anger, quick to blame, quick to avoid talking about important matters, quick to feel judged and criticized, etc.* The family members who trigger our whole 'neurotic keyboards will seem impossible. The ones who just trigger a button or two will seem very difficult. Families ideally should be the source of comfort, centeredness and renewal. That is impossible if one's buttons are too often triggered by those who are supposed to be loving and comforting us.

One important longtime goal of Murray Bowen, a famous family therapist, was the ability to be normal in the presence of his family of origin. He achieved that goal only after much therapy, much training and much trial and error. Some of us fail to see beyond our family members' obvious neuroses to what Bowen saw so clearly, that we are also acting neurotically around them.

Some believe that since they get along well with work colleagues that their mate must be the cause of the stress, altercations and "lack of communication" in their relationship. Such people often fail to realize that they are acting quite differently with their mates than they are with work colleagues. (This seems to happen more with women because they often have more satisfying friendships outside their primary spouse relationship with which to compare.) Those prone to judging and blaming are often convinced their spouse must be the one most responsible for all the problems, failing to see that their own judging and blaming are a major part of the problem.

MOTHERS CAN BE SEXIST TOO

I recently spoke with a mother who called herself a feminist. She told of how she and her female friends would never have male baby-sitters for their children because of the likelihood of physical or sexual abuse. Obviously her ideas lump men in a sexist way as abusers and molesters. What do you think her children and her friends' children are learning from their mothers' behavior? They are learning that men cannot be trusted, that men can't take care of children, that men are louts, etc. This is incredibly sexist, and it is the women who are promulgating the sexist message. They are causing trauma in both their male and female children with such messages. Their children will struggle for years overcoming such sexist messages.

Some surveys show that over half the mothers of today are reluctant to allow full child-rearing participation by the fathers, because "the fathers just wouldn't do it right." I wonder what such women would say about a CEO today remarking that "women don't belong in the CEO's chair because women just wouldn't do it right"? That CEO would be an immediate target of protest.

I think there is more involved in women being protective of their child-rearing status than just whether the father would do it right. Consider the power and increased self-esteem that the average woman feels while raising children. Many women would say that the mothering role is far more important than any work role (translation: more important than work outside the home). The raising of their children is a real power trip (empowering, not necessarily unhealthy) for many women. How do men feel about raising children? Men haven't generally admitted it, but feeling weak and dependent upon their wives accurately describes the situation of many traditional males vis-a-vis child-rearing. Isn't this precisely the traditional female experience concerning money and power outside the home? Some women seem no more willing to give up their power spheres (child-rearing and the home) than some men are willing to give up their power spheres (money and work outside the home). Yet much current-day rhetoric indicates that men are the sole problem.

MANY MEN STILL ABDICATE THEIR PARENTING ROLES

Many men still underestimate the importance of and necessity for a strongly-involved male parenting role and the self-satisfaction one derives from it. This was not always the case. Until the early 1800s, most child-rearing manuals were directed at men, who then *did* have the say about child-rearing. With the advance of industrialization, the father was more and more removed from the home. The result was that mothers made more of the child-rearing decisions. Men really *lost* an important part of the human existence with this shift. Whenever we lose parts of ourselves, it acts like trauma, and we become stressed until we regain that part of ourselves.

My guess is that this loss of parenting expertise is an important factor why men do not live as long as women. For it was also in the early 1800s that women first started living longer than men. Perhaps there will be someone who will do the research here. Do fathers who are full participants in raising their children live longer than fathers who leave such matters to their wives?

No matter the results of such longevity research, parental abdication by men remains a root cause of many of our society's ills. At all levels of schooling, on television, and from both women and men, there needs to be increased and persistent demands for male parenting responsibility. Many movies and television programs are now often showing the joys and pleasures of male parenting, and schools are now providing much-needed parenting training. Millions of women *are* now loosening a few parental reins. Millions of men *are* now emotionally available to their children. We *have* come a long way. We *can* celebrate what we have accomplished as a society without forgetting that there is more to be done.

WORKING MOMS - ARE THEIR KIDS OK?

Yes, research shows that children of working mothers do as well as those with stay-at-home mothers.* Mom's increased self-esteem and aliveness seem to counteract any ill effects that might result from a loss in her availability. (Of course, she must still choose child care well and be concerned about ensuring quality time with her children.)

On the other hand, children of divorce statistically do not do well.

CHILDREN OF DIVORCE HAVE PROBLEMS

Statistics show that children of divorce have many more problems than those children who do not suffer the divorce trauma.* Therefore, it seems that as a society we ought to be taking steps to reduce divorce and the effects of divorce, required steps such as: increased waiting periods for marriage, increased barriers to marriage, increased waiting periods for divorce, couple's mediation before divorce, couple's therapy before divorce, individual therapy for the parents before divorce, parenting classes on the effects of divorce, therapy for children of divorce, etc.

There are those who might like to make divorce nigh impossible, as it was earlier in this century. But I disagree. That led to much parental staying together that was more harmful to many of those children than divorce would have been.

*Children Begin by
Loving Their Parents; As
They Get Older They
Judge Them; Sometimes
They Forgive Them.*

Oscar Wilde

LATCHKEY CHILDREN DON'T DO AS WELL

Not surprisingly, studies have shown that children with significant amounts of time with no adult supervision (often called latchkey children) demonstrate more delinquent and antisocial behavior than their supervised peers. Given their obvious capabilities for *some* independence, they need activity leaders; and a ratio of 10-20 children to one activity leader is feasible. Thus, the solution to the latchkey problem does not entail vast sums of money. There *are* many communities that are now providing such services in after-school programs that are relatively affordable. Money spent today on such a program would more than pay for itself later on because of lower crime rates.

If such after-school programs are not available, then parents may need to reexamine the usual alternatives of relatives, trading with other parents, paid-for activities, paid child care, or split schedules for the two parents. (An alternative for one tow truck driver was to bring his two children with him when out on a tow. I wonder how many companies would allow such? Perhaps companies could change their rules and allow such employees to pay for required additional insurance.) Also, with the explosion of horrific commutes, computers, modems and home work stations, many companies are willing to try out working-at-home arrangements. Unhappily, there are still companies (and other employers such as government agencies) who have yet to realize it may be in their best interests to provide such special arrangements.

THE SEARCH FOR APPROVAL

So widespread is this search for approval that it draws little notice. It is a trait that typically has its roots in both real wants and neurotic wants. (Adult neurotic wants = adult wants caused by leftover feelings from childhood.) Most of us really do want to be appreciated and liked. Therefore, some bending of ourselves to others' wishes is to be expected from all of us. Yet, difficulty arises because one of our childhood strategies was to try to get the most from our parenting figures. The strategy caused us to twist ourselves in any way possible that would give us their approval, which most of us, as children, mistook for love. This childhood bending has caused most of us to be out of touch with some of our real wants. We often deny our real wants.

Should Exam. For a few minutes list all the "shoulds" you can think of that you have for both others and yourself. Do this now before reading further .... The fewer you can find, the happier you are. Had you ever considered that your use of the word *should* is an attempt to lay your own (or your parents') trip on others? Be on the lookout for the word *should*. For it usually shows that one is passing on automatically some unexamined ideas.* Go back over your list. Can you drop a few of them? Each one of them represents a search for parental approval without complete personal authenticity. (It is this author's goal <u>never</u> to feel as if another person *should* do something or not.) Every *should* you have for others is an ounce of unhappiness for you, also a barrier between yourself and others.

Trying for others' approval is an unhappy venture in adulthood, for it usually boomerangs. I suggest a personal goal of dropping your <u>needs</u> for others' approval. The process of achieving that goal is typically long, yet definitely worth the resulting yield of happiness dividends.

THE ELDERLY

The role of the elders in our society has changed dramatically in the last 30 years. Physically, many are in their own living spaces instead of being in a home with their children and grandchildren. They have the money to live by themselves that they did not have years ago. Their children/ grandchildren often have less money, for there has been a significant shift in disposable income toward senior citizens in the past 30 years. The gain in autonomy for senior citizens, on the one hand, has been a boon for their mental health. On the other hand, they have not all been successful at finding a meaningful life away from children and grandchildren. This has caused them much distress, unhappiness and poor health. (The down-side for their children's families has been the loss of another parenting figure for children, the loss of household help and the loss of money.)

For those getting to be very old, it is a major difficult step to realize that their path is to be "selfish and self-centered" as they review what has happened in their lives. Some of them ask the question, "Why am I still here?" The answer (from a higher-self/reincarnation framework) could be couched in the phrase *growth opportunities:*

"You have no excuse now for failing to examine many of your old ideas and beliefs, because you don't have to perform for others now. Therefore, you are freer to explore new ways of thinking and feeling. You have the opportunity to let go of judgments, to be present in the moment (because you don't have to go elsewhere), to decide to love the people around you no matter what, to be exactly who you are (i.e., be authentic), and to be grateful."

All of the above are traits commonly exhibited by contented people. The elderly, being autonomous with time on their hands, have many personal growth opportunities.** This makes their higher selves jump for joy in anticipation. On the other hand, growth is often difficult and the elderly might like to utter, along with the rest of us, "more @#$%^ growth opportunities."

Did God or your-higher-self select your family as your best teachers? If you are still bothered by a few family members, perhaps you haven't learned all that they have to teach.

---

* See Appendix A

**Possible additions to your I-WANT-LIST (see Appendix C):
      I want to communicate better with this family member_____.
      I want to eliminate my own search for others' approval.

*How do you and I contribute
to the violence that is all
around us? We are more a part
of it than we would like
to admit.*

Chapter 17

Values & Violence

HOW DO I CONTRIBUTE
TO THE ADDED VIOLENCE?

"How do I contribute?" is a question that each of us must answer. For we are the ones who are creating, tolerating and contributing to the violence we see around us. It is not just "out there" where the problems are. For if there are specific people most to blame, we are they. The essential causes of the *increased* widespread violence we see in this society seem to me to be threefold:

(1)One important cause of the added violence is a recently popular parenting strategy that avoids authoritarian/ supervisory messages. This avoidance often causes children to fear genuine authority or be insensitive to others. Children receiving this parenting often lack respect for others' rights and are sensitive only to their own wants (see previous chapter). This leads to gangs to compensate for loss of family unity and is fertile ground for violence, for the "only important thing is what I want."

(2)A recently popular parenting strategy sets up children for violence by teaching them unhappiness (see next section).

(3)Recently popular values and unhappy spiritual beliefs being taught to children by both parents and society help multiply the violence (more later in this chapter).

Our society has always been violent. It was partly in response to this longstanding violence that newer parenting strategies developed. It does seem that there are great potentials for these new parenting strategies, once the problems are ironed out. We may need to refine these strategies by reclaiming *parts* of the old ways (see *Traumatizing Children* in previous chapter).

TEACHING OUR CHILDREN TO BE UNHAPPY

How many times have you seen a two-year-old in the supermarket demanding something and then throwing a tantrum when it was not instantaneously provided? Supermarket onlookers often blame today's parents "for doing something wrong to that poor little two-year-old. That poor child is so unhappy, so obviously the parent is wrong. Are you abusing that child?"

The truth of the tantrum is that it is phony. It is manipulative behavior. We are teaching the two-year-olds that the proper response when you don't get what you want is to get unhappy. This causes both us and them untold unhappiness. Life is full of not getting what we want. We have a choice to be happy not getting what we want or to be unhappy about it. (See Chapter 8 for more on this.) Today, most of us are unhappy when things don't go our way. Do you want that unhappiness? This unhappy thinking process is one important root cause of the added violence in our society today. (When coupled with a lack of conscience about another's rights, this thinking will allow me to steal your new car, just because I want it.)

The two-year-old is a well-known pinnacle of anti-authoritarian behavior. We have changed our responses to them. Instead of swatting them, we are now trying to reason with them or to elicit their compassion. Many two-year-olds are incapable of either reason or compassion. Nor is swatting them the best answer for most. There are several possible solutions, depending upon the parents and children involved. One possible approach is that two-year-olds can be taught that they choose their responses in the supermarket. "You can choose to be unhappy and throw a tantrum or you can choose to be happy thinking about where we are going next." (Of course, they will test out such a change in parenting strategy with several tantrums.) Giving in to the manipulative tantrum, on the other hand, sets them up for future unhappiness and tendencies toward violence.

OUR VALUES & SPIRITUAL BELIEFS HELP CAUSE THE VIOLENCE

Many years ago our population generally believed in good, evil, heaven and the devil. Punishment was expected in the hereafter for all the sins committed on this earthly plane. Few were willing to risk roasting in hell forever when by acting nice one could avoid such a fate. Today, however, believing in just one chance at this incredibly "unjust" world often leads to "reaching for the gusto" even if that means doing others physical or monetary harm. "Why not be violent and greedy if there is nothing to fear? The criminal justice system will probably not catch me. Even if it does, at least I will have had the momentary pleasure of power or money."

How many of us believe there is punishment in the hereafter? Christian religions believe there is punishment for sins in this life. Similarly, the idea of karma, (paying back in future lives for wrongdoings this time around) influences the 25% of us who believe in reincarnation. It has become unfashionable to talk of paying for one's sins. Perhaps the 75% or more of us, who do believe that wrongdoings will be paid back, need to vocally object to the widespread media bias against such a belief. Just because it is unfashionable in the media does not mean that that it is undesirable. Continued promulgation of such a belief held only by a minority of the population seems to me to be a definite factor in the continuation of our society's violence.

It has become fashionable to violate laws because they are inconvenient. This is a slippery slope, for more and more often it is not just exceeding 55mph but on to inflating a few income tax deductions (convincing ourselves everyone else does it), to claiming that your group has mistreated mine (so I'll rob you or beat you), and to going after whatever I want in a violent way with no regard for others' rights (because I have been mistreated). We lose an ounce of integrity every time we disobey the 55mph law, every time we inflate a tax deduction, every time we lie, etc. _Personal authenticity and integrity are goals that are important if we are ever to find some inner contentment._ Current societal laws and values do not make that easy for anyone to achieve. Personal authenticity and integrity are not always convenient.

THE NUMBING PROCESS

While the preceding sections in this chapter emphasized causes of the _increased_ violence in our society, the original levels of violence were already high. These next sections provide additional suggestions for reducing these levels significantly.

Millions of us make the situation worse by emotionally harming (numbing) our children (as we were so harmed as children by our parents). We demand that our children swallow their hatreds for us, causing them to displace

*As Regards Conscience
God Has Done
an Uneven and Careless
Piece of Work.*
Sigmund Freud

them on to current targets like African-Americans, white males, gays, fundamentalists and women. We numb ourselves and our children (1)by making insensitivity the norm, (2)by making ourselves too often "be nice", (3)by circumcising our males, (4)by teaching our boys that to be a man means to be tough, (5)by teaching our girls to be asexual and to deny anger, etc. All these parental (and societal) teachings make us insensitive to parts of ourselves. We numb out as we try to please our parents and society.*

This numbing/ traumatizing process (described in Chapter 3) is almost universal in this society. And our "inner childs" are furious at being so numbed out! Typically, we displace our furiousness at being so numbed on to safer current targets, thus never resolving the issue for ourselves. (Rage at current targets is safer than facing our childhood rage.) Our hatred will continue on and on. If our numbing is significant enough, we will consider violence (or death or injury or pain) to be "no big deal."

A most important question is, "How do I contribute to the numbing process?" How am I still numbing my sensitivity, sexuality, anger, hatred, tears and love? If I am still displacing my rage, anger and hatreds on to safer targets of today, I am part of the violence problem. If I am still numbed, I am contributing to the continuation of violence; and I will not be maximally effective in changing others.

This is another case of "think globally, act locally." My work first is to face my own emotional numbing, including its violent and not-so-violent causes. Then I'll be much more effective in changing my parenting, the schools, television and society. This author considers numbing to be a massive human problem that will only start changing when each of us becomes more aware of our personal numbness.

HOW DO WE CONTRIBUTE
TO THE HOMELESS PROBLEM?

Psychologically, homelessness provides many of us with a constant unwanted reminder that our childhood homes were often a place of pain and emptiness instead of comfort and love. Many of us grew up, in truth, psychologically homeless despite the physically-comfortable buildings in which we might have resided. When we finally are ready to face and let go that old childhood pain (of being psychologically homeless), then we will be more effective in solving the homeless problem we see "out there" today.

One popular view has it that the homeless problem is caused by a lack of jobs. I don't agree. I think that it is our fears that make us so ineffective in dealing with the homeless, our fears that we might wind up homeless too if we lose our jobs. It is a major role of government to ease fears of citizens. So far, governmental bodies, private agencies and the citizenry have been squabbling ineffectively without making any changes that would remove citizens' fears of homelessness. Such inaction keeps our fears alive and the homeless problem unsolved.

The homeless problem is aided and abetted by those of us with apartments or homes. The inhumanity of not providing shelter for our citizens is obvious. Why do we put up with it? It is essential that this shelter provides three things: warmth, dryness and safety. Yet we are squabbling over down-the-road items such as whether drugs/ alcohol, joblessness, or failed families are the root cause. The root cause is not relevant for people who presently are cold, wet and in danger of being mugged. We must provide the opportunity for shelter first. Solutions are not that difficult, but they involve allowing housing in NIMBY (Not In My Back Yard) locations, and small rooms that don't meet minimum size requirements of local building codes.

Our society traditionally had shacks on the edge of town. With our building codes we have eliminated most of these shacks and placed their occupants on the streets. We cannot afford to solve all their problems or to provide spacious housing. Two-way construction is one solution, providing the homeless with small rooms that could be converted back and forth between use as housing and use as storage during times of less homelessness. Many homeless people rent storage spaces today. We can afford to provide small, warm, dry, and safe housing for every person who wants it. If we did, this would enable perhaps 40% of today's homeless to solve their other problems themselves at no further cost to society. It is up to us to tell the homeless advocates, our NIMBY neighbors, the building code legislators, and the idealists who want each homeless person in a spacious apartment, "Quit bickering and solve the problem effectively, humanely. Start doing it now."

The possibility of homelessness is leading many of us to (1)unhappy compromises of integrity concerning work, (2)lying and cheating behavior and (3)a wealth of fear. All three of these contribute strongly to the climate of violence, not just out there in the streets but in our homes as we teach our children to be fearful and unethical.

VERBAL BASHING CAN LEAD TO VIOLENCE

In the best of all possible worlds verbal bashing would make no difference to levels of societal violence. However, when certain men who feel so verbally incompetent (in comparison with women) get verbally bashed, they don't respond verbally. They take it inside, and it tends to erupt later as violence. These men are not OK. Their behavior is in no way excusable. They need help, and they are most definitely ill. Their levels of violence are harmful to others and to themselves. To verbally bash them unfortunately has the effect of increasing their levels of violence.

Some women seem to have forgotten how women gained poor self-esteem. Women incorporated and partially (or wholly) believed all the physical and verbal putdowns of the female gender by both men and women. In their current anger at past mistreatment, a few women are sometimes doing something similar (giving out bashing putdowns), that unexpectedly wind up increasing societal levels of physical violence. "Do unto others..." is a good motto here for all. Don't bash verbally, except briefly in therapy or by yourself.

OPPORTUNITIES TO CHANGE THE VIOLENCE

Quick fix ideas proliferate. We keep trying to blame one group such as movies, television or macho males! But these are really minor players in the violence problem. Violent behavior is the result of many different problems: poor parenting, poor criminal conscience-building, poor self-esteem, loss of feeling, fear of being soft or vulnerable, rage at the wrong target, identification with a violent parent, incorporation of violent parental/ TV messages, etc. But the wealth of causes does not mean that significant societal changes cannot be accomplished. Some suggested strategies follow.

1. As described earlier in this chapter, we can reevaluate our current parenting. We need to stop teaching our children to be unhappy, we need to place more value on personal integrity and we need to reduce societal numbing. These are all major causes of the violence we see today.

2. We need many more free editorials on children's TV about personal values. What is right and wrong? Schools all over the country have recently found that commonly held values can be taught to students in school and that the groups involved (parents, school personnel and politicians) can come to agreements about what values should be taught. Without values, we tend to

I so desire

to conduct the affairs of

this administration that if at the end

when I come to lay down the reins

of power, I have lost every friend on

earth, I shall have at least one friend

left, and that friend shall be

down inside me.

Abraham Lincoln 1864

have low self-esteem that we hope to rectify by gaining power over another. It doesn't work. (While television and movie violence are current scapegoats for societal violence, it is doubtful that violence in these two media makes too much difference - see previous chapter.)

3. A similar suggestion to one I made in the last chapter (that children be given more authoritarian messages on television) is: I suggest that criminals in jail receive conscience-building messages over loudspeakers several times daily. "It is wrong to steal. It is wrong to harm someone else. It is wrong to rape. Etc." Many of today's criminals never received such clear messages as children, and there is much evidence today that we as adults can often heal ourselves by giving ourselves the healthy messages we never received as children. (Obviously, this would not reform most criminals but it could make a significant difference in number of crimes later committed.)

4. For neighborhoods that have been taken over by gangs or drugs, we need to mobilize the army, the national guard, the marines and neighboring police forces to saturate such neighborhoods with good guys for a few weeks or months. The non-police don't have to do police work. They just have to essentially camp out so that the bad guys depart or lie low. Let the citizens come together in such safer circumstances, and they will then become much more effective combating any future takeover attempts of their neighborhood by gangs or drug dealers. Citizens will be out in force with video cameras and be much more assertive toward those with criminal tendencies once they experience a safer neighborhood. And those involved in criminal activities may change some of their behavior. Witness the gangs in Los Angeles who stopped killing one another for a time after the riots triggered by the Rodney King bashing verdict. (Yes, I know there were many influences that caused that gang change, but the presence of temporary added neighborhood safety for citizens had much to do with citizen pressure on those gangs to change.)

5. Every state needs to study the current Hawaiian social service system, which seems to have eliminated almost all child abuse in those families serviced.* The Hawaiian program is based upon *training and educating parents.* If your spouse is abusing you or your children (or you are), then you need to take action. Take that action now - call the authorities, get help and press all appropriate charges. Even if you and your children survive the current abuse, your children as grownups will probably be violent themselves or suffer violence from others unless you take action now. Over years, abuse often follows a well-known increasingly-violent pattern starting with physical threats, then hitting, beating up, weapons use and finally murder. Stop the cycle early, while there is still a chance for yourself and your children.

6. <u>We all need to understand the role of hatred, its virtual universality in small children, and the skewed emergence of child hatred against targets of today.</u> We will not be effective in dealing with others' violence while there is so much child violence within most of us. Denying our hatreds was part of our learned numbing process as children. Whatever we have numbed can erupt in violence whenever it gets triggered.

7. It seems to me that the psychological skewness of the hot debate about weapons has to do with self-esteem. <u>Those wanting weapons often feel weak but are unable to admit it, or they have a very unhappy belief about how unsafe the world is</u> (see Chapter 11). Despite the current impasse, the gun situation in this society seems about to change dramatically. For as the years have passed, more and more people have come to believe in stricter and stricter gun control. With every newly reported mass murder and family murder-suicide, the opposed-to-weapons trend in the polls accelerates. The message of "when weapons are outlawed, only outlaws will have weapons" is an attempt to spread a fear message to others. The answer to that, of course, is, "But outlaws will have fewer weapons, and fewer lives will be lost." Those opposing weapons are not always neurosis-free either, in their opposition to weapons. For some are playing the victim role and are lacking in self-esteem and a spiritual system that can provide inner peace. Nevertheless, fewer lives would be lost, and we would have much less societal fear if strict weapon control were enacted. Clearly this would change the levels of societal violence, perhaps not dramatically but significantly.

8. <u>The role that governments (at all levels) play in raising the levels of violence should not be underestimated.</u> We as a society, with present levels of funding, can promise and provide necessary *basic* levels of food, clothing, personal shelter (warm, dry and safe), and medical care to all citizens. Doing so would change the level of societal violence significantly because fears of being hungry, sick or in physical danger would be significantly eased.

9. <u>So-called spiritual values that consider humans to be essentially evil/ flawed still contribute heavily to our problems with violence.</u> People who believe they are evil will act that way. Similarly, violence is promoted by the unhappy psychological notion that we are raging cauldrons that need capping. While one often finds rage and violence beneath our surfaces, it has been my experience that rage and violence are absent once childhood issues have been faced and resolved (see chapter 10).

To sum up, there are many choices we as a society can make to significantly reduce our societal violence. To some degree, we are all causing today's violence because we are avoiding some difficult personal choices. Let's make the hard choices!

HOW INGRAINED IS THE VIOLENCE?

Not that ingrained! When the gangs in Los Angeles decided to stop killing one another after the riots following the Rodney King bashing verdict, they succeeded for a time. Also, once those who are violent because of inner-child violence feel their childhood rages/ hatreds, their current levels of anger are vastly reduced. (As discussed in prior chapters, our stuffed childhood feelings, including rage, *cause* much of our current anger and violence.)

It seems to me to be a hopeful time concerning violence, provided more of us assume responsibility for making the changes to the ideas and beliefs within ourselves that contribute to the violence. This does seem to be happening!**

At our cores we seem to be peaceful, creative, joyful and loving.

---

*   See Appendix A

** Possible additions to your I-WANT-LIST (see Appendix C):
      To reduce societal violence, I want to_____.
      My unhappy values that I want to change are_____.

Every Day
in Every Way
I'm Getting Better
and Better

Emile Coue`

This author says,

"Still a useful statement."

Chapter 18
Therapists & Therapies

RECOMMENDED GOAL OF THERAPY: INNER PEACE

While the dictionary defines therapy in terms of healing, there is significant disagreement about the meaning of healing in therapy. For some it implies one or more of the following: behavior change, symptom reduction, improved self-esteem or happily-ever-after. Some have therapeutic goals of a long-term committed relationship or a job with a good income (whatever $$$ that may mean). Instead of any of these goals, I suggest one longterm goal: inner peace. (This could also be phrased as happiness or contentment.)

For us to achieve inner peace, it is vital that it be a high priority goal. If it is not, we tend to flounder in the never ending seasons of our discontent. For much more on achieving happiness and inner peace congruent with the ideas of this paragraph, I strongly recommend Kaufman's *Happiness Is a Choice*. Those who do achieve contentedness seem to have traveled other growth paths to the extent that they also exhibit (1)personal authenticity, (2)a heightened ability to be present in the moment, and (3)a lack of judgments of others. To be lacking authenticity, to be often stuck in the past/ future or to be critical of others seems to prevent contentedness..

Other goals that seem reasonable may have flaws. If my unconscious lifeplan (see Chapter 8) is to meet with lifemate Jane in three years, then any therapy goal I have to meet my lifemate next week must fail. Assume my lifeplan is to work on any of my difficulties (addictions, being overweight, phobias, self-esteem, relationship struggles, etc.) with a particular person five years from now. Then therapy in that particular area today will fail if I attempt to resolve any difficulties that are a part of my *future* lifeplan. Some so-called "failures in therapy" may be nothing of the sort. They may be evidence of an overriding lifeplan that doesn't allow resolution of that problem now.

215

Our goals in life often require revision once we start therapy. We have all received societal training in having outer-directed goals such as money, job, car, house, relationship, status and power. Outer-directed goals are often the ones most appropriate for us, particularly before we reach our thirties. As we grow older, many of our goals need to change to inner-directed *being* goals (see next paragraph). It is important not to judge others' goals as wrong. There are 50-year-olds who may be *appropriately for them* pursuing money, status, etc., as part of a higher-self lifeplan for the pursuit of money or status.

Adult goals that will usually give many of us more contentment and happiness are inner-directed *being* goals: being contented, being authentic, being accepting, being present, being honest, being aware, being powerful (in positive ways), being influential (in positive ways), being creative, being sexual, being loving, being grateful, being ourselves, enjoying laughter, enjoying humor and honoring our emotions.

DON'T GIVE ALL YOUR PERSONAL POWER TO A THERAPIST

There is a strong tendency among those who seek out therapists to be looking for too many answers from them. "All I have to do is find the right therapist, who will then fix everything. I'll accept uncritically what my therapist says and attempt to act the way my therapist thinks best." This type of thought process (often unconscious) is all too common, even among therapists themselves concerning their own therapists. Most of my recent clients have been other therapists and their family members. Initially, some therapists even ask such things as, "What should I do?" and "What is best for me?". These questions reveal that such clients are giving away too much of their personal power. Lurking within them is a perpetual feeling of poor self-esteem and a neverending sense of inadequacy in knowing what is right for themselves.*

What is needed instead is to make the therapist into an assistant rather than a guru. In many ways this book can help you do just that. Understanding a bit about trauma, psychology and therapy (just the few pages in Chapter 3) will help significantly. Finding out more about one's problems via the questionnaire in Appendix A will give a better sense of what might be accomplished in therapy, in plain language instead of psychobabble.

THERAPISTS WILL DISAGREE
WITH THESE WORDS

Like the rest of today's society, therapists are a diverse group with quite different ideas about almost any topic you might raise. Several of my colleagues heard the title of this book and responded from a framework of, "Such a book will take clients away from me." Instead, this book could well propel people into getting help because they read that a particular feeling or emotion or set of unhappy ideas can be changed! If they can't change by self-help methods, they will seek out professional help. This might translate to more clients for therapists, not less, because more than 90% of the population is not currently in therapy. For most of those in treatment, a self-help book such as this one is most unlikely to end therapy because they *do* need help from a therapist. But it could encourage them to negotiate a shift in therapy emphasis to areas that might have been overlooked. Good!

Colleagues will disagree with much of what has been written in this book. The "thinking" ideas in Chapter 8 will tend to be wholly accepted only by those strongly involved with "thinking" therapies such as Rational-Emotive, Option, and Cognitive-Behavioral. Many of those "thinking" ideas will be rejected (at times scornfully) by therapists with other approaches. Similarly, many "emotional" ideas in Chapters 9 & 10 will be rejected by therapists with different views. Many of the spiritual ideas in Chapter 11 will likely be rejected by most therapists except *transpersonal* therapists. All these therapist disagreements confuse consumers in their searches for therapists.

FINDING A THERAPIST -
SETTING THERAPY GOALS

There is no one therapy treatment that is considered standard, as there would be for your ruptured appendix. (A reminder here about the Maori drawing in Appendix B - that drawing may help you figure out the type/ focus of therapy that could be most beneficial to you today.)

If you are a planning type, you will be seeking out information about a prospective therapist. Do so. You will feel better. Often you will do better than the impulsive therapist shopper. For trust in and rapport with a therapist are often (but not always) important to the success of the therapy. You can often find out that information beforehand. Trust yourself. A specific approach you

It Is Impossible To Live Pleasureably Without Living Wisely, Well and Justly, and Impossible to Live Wisely, Well and Justly Without Living Pleasureably.

Epicurus 341-270 B.C.

could take involves the "I-Want" footnotes at the end of the chapters in this book. Using these footnotes and Appendix C as a guide, make a list of "I-Wants" that are important to you. Reduce your list to three or four of your most important "I-Wants." Take this list to discuss with prospective therapists. These might become your **therapy goals**.

If you are an impulsive type, you probably will throw darts at the telephone listings of therapists or seek out your friend's therapist. Careful planning is not for you. Sometimes you will do better by this method than the careful planners. For there are times when a very different therapist, one you would never select through careful planning, will be the most effective for you.

Any therapist is likely to be an improvement over none at all if you are in significant/ severe distress. If you discover you have chosen the wrong therapist, find someone different.

LIFE IS LUMPY

Life is like lumpy gravy. Unfortunately, life-gravy has one nasty habit. It keeps producing more lumps. You are the chef. Your choices are to mash the lumps, chew the lumps, smooth the lumps or avoid the lumps. Permanent avoidance of lumps makes emotional, physical, and psychological symptoms worse. You may hire an assistant chef (therapist) to help. If the lumps seem impossible, or the same lumps keep reappearing, or you are severely distressed by one or more of them, then you had best stop *avoiding* your lumps. If your distress is mild, try this book or others, talk to friends or join a support group.

If your distress is severe or self-help approaches prove ineffective, you need to consider hiring a lump specialist (i.e., a paid therapist) as an assistant.

CHANGES, SELF-GROWTH AND THERAPY DON'T ALWAYS TICKLE

Therapy usually does make you feel better. But that does not imply that you will feel better immediately. In some ways therapy is like going to a dentist with a toothache. Sometimes you get the added pain of a novocaine needle, of drilling or of sore gums afterwards before all the mouth pain, including that of the original toothache, disappears. Similarly, facing psychological problems means that one's symptoms sometimes seem to get worse. Of course! This is natural. Our defenses keep us from what we don't want to face. The threat of having to face these unwanted issues raises our anxiety and thus increases our symptoms.

Aloneness is a routine feature of self-growth, particularly in the specific area of current decision. Difficult situations, ideas and feelings immediately arise once one decides to change; aloneness is often especially difficult. A woman, in her attempts to break out of the housewife mold, may be faced with how to be assertive, how to face anger, how to express herself in job situations, and how to or even whether to choose a new occupation that might not be conventionally female. All these choices will usually result in many feelings of being alone and without much support as she finds her way along her own individual path of growth. Her old friends may not be there for her, and even if they are, they may not be of much assistance. For they need the same growth she is having to find for herself. I do not recommend retreating in the face of feeling so stranded. Some aloneness must be faced if satisfactory self-esteem is ever to be achieved. This is a significant aspect of how we gain self-esteem - we do our own thinking and come up with our own ideas and paths. It may be necessary to force oneself to stay with aloneness instead of retreating into past habit patterns. (Men also back away from much aloneness, particularly that aloneness associated with grief and hopelessness in their childhoods.)

One unpopular psychological truism (also Earth School truism) is that once I start to face and overcome problem X, then my next problem, Y, will often raise its problematic head. Y may be my most painful and difficult problem ever. Just having Y in the background may raise my anxiety and symptoms to a fever pitch. If I fall into the feeling-good trap, I am likely to conclude that it must be wrong for me because of the added stress. If so, I resume my old unhappy ways.

VENTILATION IS NOT ENOUGH

One important ingredient of many talk therapies is full expression (ventilation) of one's problems and difficulties. Instead of cursing out the boss or my child, I attempt to fully ventilate my thoughts, ideas, words, frustration, rage and angst in my therapy session. Thus, I avoid blurting it out at targets for whom prudence might dictate silence.

As with all good things, however, ventilation can be overworked and overused. I have met a few clients who have tried to elevate ventilation into being 100% of what therapy is all about. They attempted to turn each session into a long-winded complaint session. "This is awful" and "I am a victim" are the common beliefs that predominate. Those clients were accustomed to using therapy as a feel-good-temporarily tool. They were not appreciative when confronted with the addictive qualities of their behavior. Ventilation is usually just a beginning step in therapy.

SUFFERING SMARTER IS DUMB

There is a process that unfortunately happens with too much regularity in some therapies. Emphasis on insight often results in insight becoming the therapeutic goal. Such a goal often just leads to rational explanations of my lousy behavior or my stressed-out condition. "I do this or am distressed by that because I was abused by Dad. *Of course* I am distressed by that. *Of course* I do that." My insight may be valid, for Dad's abuse may be the original trauma or learning that fostered today's problems. And yes, I would always agree that the reaction I just had (or the action I just took) was *exactly* right for me based upon my entire life history. I then need to ask a most unpopular question, "Do I want to act or react the same way next time?". Such a question implies that change is very possible, and my first reaction may often be disbelief that such change is possible. (See Chapter 8.)

The bright focus on insight all too often causes a shadow to be cast over the more appropriate therapeutic goals of *not being stressed that way anymore* and *not acting that way anymore*. Understanding distress or the etiology of lousy behavior is often just a step along the path toward changing actions and relieving distress. Those who stay with insight usually have many insights but are still suffering with the difficulties that originally propelled them into therapy. I call this "suffering smarter," but it does seem dumb.

While the psychoanalytic path is known for its emphasis on insight, it is not the only path where clients *sometimes* fall into the "suffering smarter" trap. Intellectual clients and therapists seem to be the ones most prone to "suffering smarter." By clinging to insight, intellectual techniques often avoid necessary (1)upset feelings, (2)unwanted impulses and (3)distasteful confusion. It is a trap that can affect almost any therapy. This implies that you, the buyer, must beware. If your insights are not leading to behavior change or to now

Happiness and unhappiness
don't just happen to
us. Happiness is a choice.

feeling OK about situations that used to be bothersome, then you are likely to be "suffering smarter." You need to evaluate what is happening in your therapy.

EACH THERAPY HAS ITS OWN LIMITS

To say that favorite therapy Brand X has limits will sometimes not be accepted by either clients or therapists following X's path. It makes sense that exploring X's areas of therapy deeply will dictate less exploration in other areas. But followers of Brand X will often label some other explorations impossible or irrelevant.

One current such "impossibility" is not impossible at all, namely the resolution of trauma from the first two years of life. One *verbally* oriented psychiatrist recently proclaimed that trauma resolution from the first two years of life was impossible. He really was right, *with his methods*. His methods were verbal, so why would one expect him to have success with *nonverbal* trauma? You may have significant trauma from your first two years. Common psychological traumas for babies are: (1)pain during birth, (2)early painful medical interventions, (3)parental addicts or abusers or (4)parental neglect of needs for prompt care. If you believe you may have such trauma, the following methods have had satisfactory success with early nonverbal trauma: Rebirthing, Primal, EMDR and some bodywork therapies (this author would recommend trying EMDR first).

Many therapists instantaneously dismiss the possibility of past life trauma. For help here, ask therapists/ hypnotists in your area if they know therapists doing this work. If past life trauma is the source of your difficulties, conventional therapy will not be of much help. Conventional therapy will often just label you resistant. Do not rush to get past life therapy; for most never seem to need it. Even fewer need it in the beginning stages of therapy. (See Chapter 11 for more about this.)

ALL PEOPLE DO NOT HAVE
THE SAME MOTIVATIONS

For example, the most common type of therapist really wants to help and is strongly motivated by service. Well and good! Helping people to change and heal is the essence of being a therapist. Other basic satisfactions (besides service) are prevalent in society too, and they are as vital to other folks as service is to the typical therapist. Seven basic satisfactions (See *Messages from Michael*) are:

Helping Creating Persuading Learning Mastering Inspiring Expressing

Which of these give *you* the most satisfaction? Do you want to increase its frequency? We are not all the same in this regard. Do not try to become a helper (or other role) to please your therapist or your family. The other satisfactions are no less important to society. Following someone else's basic satisfaction just leads to unhappiness.

Another basic difference among us is the basic relating style each of us demonstrates around other people. Famous early therapists such as Karen Horney talked of three styles of relating: (1)going towards, (2)going against and (3)going away from. People (not this author) often believe that the first is normal and the latter two are dysfunctional.

The most common style (probably 90+% of us) is to go toward other people, wanting to relate, wanting to be with them, wanting to interact. One of the two "incorrect" styles is the Saddam Hussein style of going against other people, tweaking their noses, trying to get them upset, acting destructively, being a sociopath or psychopath, etc. The other "incorrect" style of going away from people is the hermit, the schizoid, the loner. The style of going toward others is usually easier for those with that inherent style than for those encountering the difficulties inherent in the other two styles.

That does not mean that one should be converting the other two styles. Instead, the best goal for 'going against' people might be to find their own right level of 'going against'. Therapists could help such people to do so - accepting the consequences of their behavior, being OK with rejection, etc. Similarly, the best goal of therapy for loners might be for them to find their own appropriate level of aloneness. If "going against" and "going away from" are basic needs or lifeplans for a particular individual, then any therapy that tries to erase such behavior will fail. Could this be a reason why there is such therapy failure with sociopaths and loners? While I would agree that these two types are likely to suffer more psychologically and to have many more symptoms, I suspect that their lifeplans are as much responsible for such personal relating styles as their past trauma. If their lifeplans are the cause, then any attempt to change their relating styles will fail.

FEELINGS

Many therapists have elevated feelings almost to godlike status. They *are* extremely important. If you cannot feel, you are most definitely psychologically unhealthy. Also, the more you cannot feel, the unhealthier you are. There has been much *essential* therapy emphasis on learning to feel and to express emotions.

Relatively noncontroversial is the idea that if I am blocking an uncomfortable emotion, then its expression will usually ease my discomfort. The ease, however, will be temporary if the emotion was either improperly directed at the wrong target or was the wrong emotion itself (see Chapter 9). More controversial is the idea that if I have an uncomfortable feeling, then I can always change that feeling by changing my thinking as discussed earlier in Chapter 8.

Some therapists and clients have spent so much energy regaining feelings and emotions after repressing/ denying them for decades that they lose sight of the fact that feelings and emotions are transitory. They stay stuck in the same unhappy feelings over and over. The basis for the cognitive styles of therapy (such as Option, Rational-Emotive and Cognitive-Behavioral) is that such uncomfortable feelings and emotions can often be made to go away just by changing one's thinking (see Chapter 8).

Feelings are vital, but if the end result of feeling them is not the feeling of calmness, you may be stuck.

THERAPISTS IN THERAPY

The majority of my clients for the past two years have been other therapists coming to me because I advertised that I could help them *resolve* difficulties they may have had for some time. These difficulties seem to have resisted many prior therapy efforts. For some problems therapists are stuck in Stage I *denial* as described in Chapter 4 (denying problems such as unhappiness-causing spiritual systems). For other problems they are stuck in the *blaming* Stage II (blaming their children, their spouses or their parents for many upset feelings). They may be stuck making the same unhappy choices over and over (the helplessness of Stage II). Fortunately, most have been willing to do the work necessary to move through the stuck places.

Well-being Is Attained
by Little and Little,
and Nevertheless It Is No
Little Thing Itself
Zeno 4th-3rd Century BC

To expect your therapist to be without any hangups or difficulties is unrealistic. Therapists too are here on Earth School to learn psychological lessons. Often the best therapy is done by therapists who have traveled your problem route. But that does not mean they are problem-free. "A therapist can only take you as far as he/ she has gone" is an adage worth remembering when you interview potential therapists.

There is an old widely circulated belief that therapists become therapists in an attempt to resolve their own problems. There is some truth to that, but it is not an either-or situation. It is a both-and situation; they become therapists to help *both* themselves *and* others. There *is* strong ethical training for therapists which emphasizes recognizing when one's own problems are in the way. Too often, people use therapist imperfection as a tool to avoid therapy, thus remaining fixated with their own lemons.

LEMON THERAPISTS

Yes, they exist, as do lemons in every other occupation. Fortunately there is usually much regulation that weeds out incompetents, reducing their numbers to a small percentage. Nevertheless, there are therapists who display various types of lemon behavior. Lemon behavior might include:

(1)Sex with clients. Report these therapists to your state board; they are likely to lose their licenses if the charges are bonafide.
(2)Taking on clients who are known to fall outside areas of expertise. Fortunately, this is a highly emphasized area of therapist ethical training. (3)Not encouraging termination of therapy when goals are reached or therapy has become ineffective. Therapist ego is in the way.

OUR SOCIETY IS ON THE *RIGHT* TRACK

Historically our society in the 1940s and 1950s was stuck in Stage I *denial*. We denied or minimized our problems as individuals and as a society. "We don't have any problems with sexism, racism, or keeping up with the Joneses." Then, during the next generation in the 60s, 70s and 80s, Stage II rebellion and blame took center stage. "You are causing my problems. You should fix yourself so that I can be happy. It is all someone else's fault why I get so many sour lemons in my life."

Now in the mid-1990s, the possibility that all those lemons need to be made into lemonade is starting to enter the consciousness of millions. We are now as a society proceeding into Stages III, IV, and V, the stages where our lemons are made into lemonade. These stages are where we individually choose to resolve our difficulties (lemons) whether anyone else makes any changes at all. It is possible and very freeing. Shirley MacLaine has done wonders for our society with her spotlight on spirituality, Roseanne too with her widespread talking about the secrets of abuse.

MISSING FROM THIS BOOK

As I review what I have included and what I have left out, what strikes me most is how much has been left out. I have failed to mention art, music, or dance therapy. I have said little about dreams, yet they can be of invaluable use both in therapy and in self-growth. I have failed to talk much about relationships and relationship therapies, particularly family therapy, often the most effective treatment. The material presented sometimes seems thin. Such is the nature of this written beast. What about important contributions from body-mind medical healers such as Dr. Deepak Chopra's *Ageless Body, Timeless Mind* and Dr. Bernie Siegel's *Love, Medicine & Miracles*? What about Louise Hay's life-transforming affirmations from *You Can Heal Your Life*? Despite what is missing, I do believe what I have written can be useful for you, the reader, in your life pursuits. It can often be used with whatever healing/ therapy method you are following.

Good luck with it.

YOUR PERFECT THERAPY

You are doing it right now, whether you read this book or throw it out, whether you hire someone to help or try it on your own for the moment, or whether you are avoiding all growth. Even if you seem to be on a bad detour, it is often useful to see that detour as necessary. To understand and accept the perfection of your present life is useful (though it may be difficult - see Chapter 8). The way you are and the way you act are perfect results of your entire life history and experience. Of course you are that way and act that way. If you don't like that perfection you may choose to change the way you are and the way you act by some personal growth method. For your life and for your growth, you are the real director, producer, makeup artist and performer. Hire assistants (i.e., paid therapists) when you need them, but consider yourself your own best therapist. For maximum happiness---

Decide to embrace-	Decide to let go of-
Appreciation and Gratefulness	Blame
Personal Authenticity	Phoniness
All Emotions (Briefly)	Stuck Emotions
The Safety of the Universe	Fear
Being in the Present	Worrying and Ruminating
Spirit	Judgments
Love	Need for Approval
All of One's Physical Body	Unhappiness

The more we can follow the prescriptions of the left-hand-column above, the closer we shall be to inner peace. Isn't inner peace really what you want?

If you make inner peace your goal,
it will develop, bit by bit.

Appendices

Appendices

(Possible Self-Help Tools While Reading This Book)

Appendix A - SELF-HELP QUIZ

This quiz is intended for those of you who enjoy quizzes in your favorite magazines. Find the "right" answers to this quiz in each chapter (page numbers are listed after each question). For maximum benefit, though such an order is certainly not essential, it is suggested that you answer all these questions before you have read much of the book. Learning from your answers as you read each chapter can be important for you. My "answers" are marked with * throughout the book. Usually they are not "right" answers, but ways of thinking and being that prove happier for people than other commonly encountered alternatives. They are opinions which in my experience have proven to be the happier answers for myself and my clients. Part of your process may be to evaluate the differences between your current answers and what I am suggesting may be happier alternatives. *Your answers are not wrong, no matter what they are.* But they may be at the root of much of your stress and unhappiness.

Introduction

T F   Most work of psychotherapy needs to be accomplished in the therapy hour. [1]

T F   The goals of a client's psychotherapy should be made by the therapist rather than by the client. [1]

T F   The therapist is paid to know what is best for his/her clients. [2]

Chapter 1 - Using This Book

T F   The more experienced your therapist, the more of your answers he/she will be able to give you. [6]

T F   For maximum health, one or more of the following may be safely ignored:
1. the body 2.the mind 3.the emotions 4.spirituality   [7]

T F   Personal choices that are popular in this society often cause us distress. [9]

T F   In therapy the client rather than the therapist is the ultimate boss. [9]

T F   To realize that there are alternatives to our lousy responses is not useful, for such knowledge typically just makes us feel worse. [12]

Chapter 2 - Gain, No Pain

T F   Before people can truly enjoy the treasures of spontaneity, creativity and laughter, it is usually necessary to first face old childhood traumas. [15]

T F   The amounts of spontaneity, creativity and fun usually are fixed within us and cannot be changed much by our efforts to overcome our ignorance. [17]

T F Goals are desirable; without them we tend to flounder. With the wrong goals we also flounder. [19]

Chapter 3 - Psychology (KISS)

T F By the age of 35, most of us are not much affected by childhood traumas. [21]

T F The symptoms of trauma are everywhere. [23]

T F Words, emotions, sensations and thoughts are often frozen by traumatic situations in areas of our minds away from conscious memory. [23]

T F Children often squelch their emotions to please parents and wind up traumatized as a result. [24]

T F Stopping our searches for others' approval will yield large dividends of happiness. [25]

T F Addictive behavior is very often used as a temporary means of reducing the stress resulting from unresolved trauma. [28]

Chapter 4 - Stages of Healing / Making Changes

T F A rest from any of our problems is evidence of our dysfunction. [32]

T F It is helpful to be self-critical along the lines of, "I'm no good." [35]

T F There is always a valid reason for procrastination. [35]

Chapter 5 - Your Body Is Not a Carcass

T F Emotional happiness will probably not be experienced to any great degree if the body is neglected. [41]

T F If we stuff our words and emotions, then our bodies also tend to shut down and become numb. [41]

T F One common feature of contented people is their ability to be in the present moment. [42]

T F The results from bodywork therapies often are significantly helped if words and emotions are incorporated into the therapy. [42]

T F It is often a significant growth experience for a man to hug another man for the first time. [45]

T F For most, reasonable fitness requires much more than 30 minutes a week. [49]

Chapter 6 - Mystery Meat

T F If I am depressed, overweight or anxiety-ridden, it would be rather foolish for me to consider allergies as a possible cause. [53]

T F Allergy reactions are obvious. [55]

T F Testing oneself for food allergy is difficult. [57]

Chapter 7 - Fat

T F Diet programs that do not include exercise will usually fail. [59]

T F You can change the speed of your metabolism by exercise. [59]

T F To start liking a food more, try eating it more often. [61]

T F Solving your psychological problems will surely solve your weight problems. [64]

T F One essential ingredient of most successful weight loss plans is the mental image of being thinner. [67]

Chapter 8 - Thinking

T F Changing how I think about people or situations will often change my emotional responses to them. [71]

T F Right/ wrong judgments make us feel good. [72]

T F It is possible to attain the ultimate in self-responsibility: specifically, if I am unhappy, then I can always change my unhappiness. [75]

T F Hurt feelings often indicate a loss of personal power. [76]

T F It is important for us to distrust impulses. [81]

T F It is natural to be unhappy when one does not get what one wants. [86]

Chapter 9 - Emotional Health = Mental Health

T F Many of us lack emotional health much of the time. [91]

T F My anger at him stems more from my *expectations* than from his actions. [92]

T F Love is a decision. [95]

T F Tears and sobbing show weakness. [98]

T F Stress is just another synonym for *fear*. [99]

Chapter 10 - Therapy 4-H Club

T F The core feelings in our trauma knots are hatred, hurt and hopelessness. [105]

T F Being out of touch with inner child hatred causes societal violence today. [109]

T F The body reacts to an imagined experience in much the same way as to a "real" experience. [111]

Chapter 11 - Spirituality (I Do Not Mean Religion)

T F The belief that our consciousness dies when our body dies causes much distress in this society. [117]

T F Your answer to the question - "What is the meaning of life?" - has little relevance to your current happiness. [121]

T F Changing a person's spiritual system of beliefs may be essential if that person is to attain inner peace. [124]

T F To believe that this is a safe universe is obviously crazy. [129]

Chapter 12 - Our Favorite Groups Have Problems Too
T F A majority today are sexist, racist or homophobic. [136]

T F Placing all the blame elsewhere excuses us from looking at ourselves. [143]

T F Those who wish to change white males today had best *fight* hard. [144]

Chapter 13 - Women & Men
T F Men and women think very differently. [148]

T F Women are the left-brained sex, men the right-brained. [151]

T F It is recommended that a man meet his spouse's housework standards. [153]

T F Genuine acceptance means that the other's foibles and failures are OK. [155]

T F Men are often insensitive to difficulties with hurt, sadness and fear. [155]

T F Women are often insensitive to difficulties with sexuality, competitiveness and anger. [158]

Chapter 14 - Work
T F Doing the work you love is an important prescription for happiness. [163]

T F Income differences between the sexes are influenced by women's choices. [167]

T F The glass ceiling is caused solely by sexism/ racism. [168]

T F For your own happiness, it is better to consider competition to be neutral. [170]

Chapter 15 - Sex
T F All who grew up in the USA have received some Puritan sexual training. [177]

T F Most gay men and lesbians *choose* consciously to be aroused by persons of the same sex. [179]

T F Our sexual feelings will tend to follow our emotionally loving feelings. [179]

T F Pornography has been shown to be very damaging to society. [181]

Chapter 16 - Families
T F Authoritarian messages are harmful to children and should be avoided. [190]

T F With our families, we are usually at our most relaxed and least skewed. [195]

T F Children of working mothers do as well as those of stay-at-home mothers. [197]

T F Children of divorce don't do as well as their peers. [197]

Chapter 17 - Values & Violence
T F Almost all of us numbed out to please parents and/or society. [207]

T F In Hawaii almost all child abuse in targeted risky populations has been stopped. [211]

233

Appendix B

The contents of this appendix are from the written works of Angeles Arrien Phd, anthropologist, healer, lecturer and author. If you wish information about Dr. Arrien's current lectures, workshops, books and tapes, please call (415) 331-5050.

MAORI DRAWING
A Cross-Cultural Diagnostic Tool

Copyright © 1987 *by Angeles Arrien Ph.D.*

BACKGROUND

What I present to you here integrates the Maori wisdom with my research and study in cross-cultural symbols. Like Western sandtray work, mandala drawing or art therapy, the Maori drawing is a way of seeing where you are in your life: physically, emotionally, mentally and spiritually. This tool (or process) was acquired during my field research among the Maoris in the late 1960s.

The traditional Maori way is to create a sacred drawing on the ground. On your birthday you would clear a spot of land as long as you are tall and as wide as your arms reach. You would groom it carefully, clearing it for your drawing. You would find a drawing stick from nature. To witness your process, your best friend would be there, also someone who is a healer. You might have brought crushed berries, flower petals, feathers, pine cones or stones to make part of the image. After meditating and quieting your spirit, you would create your drawing on the ground freely and rapidly, working in fifteen times the shadow of the sun-- or 15 minutes.

A large blank sheet of paper becomes your sacred space. Draw a large circle on your paper to define your sacred space. There is no right or wrong way for your own inner process as shown by your drawing. Trust your inner guidance. You might ritualize this creation of your drawing and consider it a healing ceremony for yourself. You might honor this time as a birthing time in your own healing process. No two drawings are alike. Each is unique. Please approach your drawing with a sense of respect for (1) your own inner process and (2) the ancient Maori wisdom that likely will be imparted to you.

SUPPLIES

Select a large piece of paper, the larger the better, along with pencil. (You also might have pens, colored markers, chalk, crayons etc., but these are not absolutely necessary.)

DOING THE DRAWING - when you are ready to begin . . . . .

1. Clear the physical space around you so that you have room to work. Clear your inner space by meditation, by relaxation or by taking a few deep breaths.

2. In your mind ask your best friend to witness your process and imagine (or pretend) that she/he is present.

3. Who is a healer for you -- someone you know personally? Someone historical? Imagine (or pretend) that the healer is present and blessing your process.

4. On your blank sheet of paper draw a large circle.

5. Now, in 15 minutes, make your drawing, placing eight listed symbols inside your drawn circle. This is sacred space, sacred time and sacred purpose. (If you have difficulty with the word *sacred*, substitute *space to be valued, time to be valued, and purpose to be valued.*) Remember that the size of each symbol means nothing here. Disengage the part of your brain that requires things to be in proportion to each other, or that they be in certain colors, and so on. Draw as if you were dreaming. The eight symbols are:

snake or serpent	**butterfly**	**flower**	**mountain**
tree	**shelter**	**path**	**bird**

6. When your drawing is complete, close your eyes for a few minutes of quiet thoughts. Memorize your drawing in your mind. Extend your appreciation to your own creativity, also to your friend and to the healer who have been witnesses.

AFTER COMPLETING YOUR DRAWING

Ideally, for the next few days keep your drawing somewhere that you can see it often. For now, let the symbols speak directly to you without interpreting them - get to know your drawing with a beginner's mind first. Let a week pass before you read further about the interpretation. Then proceed to the next page, which contains guidelines for interpreting your drawing.

Please complete your Maori drawing on preceding page before reading this page.

Interpretation of Maori Drawing

Combining traditional wisdom of the Basque and Maori cultures, and cross-cultural symbolism, we will look at your drawing in several different ways. The *location* of symbols in each of the four quadrants of your drawing will be interpreted. The *meaning* of symbols will be given. Your *process* in completing the drawing will be interpreted. Lastly, the *interaction* of symbols will be discussed.

LOCATIONS OF YOUR SYMBOLS IN QUADRANTS

Divide your Maori Drawing into four quadrants by twice folding your paper, in half and then in half again, once vertically and once horizontally. Unfold your paper. You now have your drawing divided into four quadrants, upper left and right, also lower left and right. Each quadrant represents an area of human existence: mental = upper left, spiritual = upper right, emotional = lower left, and physical = lower right.

1. The **mental** (upper left) quadrant (or "valley of the birds") concerns the mind, ideas, beliefs, thinking, and concepts.

2. The **spiritual** (upper right) quadrant (or "valley of the mountains") is the spiritual home of the great spirit and is concerned with spiritual healing and activity.

3. The **emotional** (lower left) quadrant (or "valley of the flowers") is the emotional clear sea and is associated with the heart and emotional nature.

4. The **physical** (lower right) quadrant (or "valley of the trees") is the physical home of the earth and is associated with your body, relationships, finances and health.

In general, the quadrant with the least symbols represents a need for a place of reflection or quietude. The quadrant with the most symbols represents the most activity and conscious development. **Balance is key.** When you look at your drawing, what quadrant is most empty, most full? Do you agree with the interpretation that you are not very actively involved today with your emptiest quadrant? Do you want to change that level of involvement? Do you want less involvement with your busiest quadrant? (Do not judge hastily, for there are times in life when a major focus on one quadrant might be most appropriate.)

Symbols that occur in two or more quadrants are integrating factors that strengthen the connections between those aspects of yourself represented by the quadrants involved (i.e., mental/spiritual/ emotional/physical aspects).

MEANINGS OF SYMBOLS - (snake, bird, etc.)

If you duplicated or multiplied any symbols (for example, five birds instead of one), this shows an area of your life that wants to be intensified or experienced in multiple ways; or it represents a significant process that wants to be experienced in multiple parts of your life.

If you added extra symbols, perhaps a lake or an animal (or anything else beyond the eight symbols given), these are ways you already know how to heal yourself.

Your largest symbol is that with which you have the most identity and is also the key to your well-being. Your smallest symbol shows what is just starting or beginning but is still unknown or not yet in full awareness.

The **snake** is a symbol of transformation, regeneration, renewal, healing, old wisdom, overcoming fear, personal power, sensuality and sexuality. You might interpret the snake in your drawing as follows: "I am in the process of shedding an old (mental/ spiritual/ emotional/ physical) skin." *{Pick the appropriate word(s) depending upon which quadrant(s) your snake is in.}* Or perhaps, "I am in the process of overcoming fears of my (mental/ spiritual/ emotional/ physical) nature."

The **flower** depicts your unfoldment, your quality of opening to other people and to yourself. The flower in your drawing suggests you tend to do this (mentally/ spiritually/ emotionally/ physically). *{Pick the appropriate word(s) depending upon which quadrant(s) your flower(s) is(are) in.}* Is your flower in full bloom (fully open to others) or just a bud preparing to bloom (not yet fully open to others)? Flowers are universally used for courtship, marriage, birth and death.

The **tree** is a natural, organic symbol of who you are and your evolutionary growth process. You may or may not be aware of it, because it is the deep unconscious. The tree is a picture of your life over time. The roots symbolize your past. The trunk or core of the tree is you in the present. The branches and foliage are the future (what you are reaching for and how harvestable you think your goals are). You might interpret the tree trunk in your drawing as showing present-day strong, perhaps unconscious, involvement in a (mental/ spiritual/ emotional/ physical) area of your life. A spring tree suggests new experiences. A summer tree shows full fruiting. A fall tree shows something is being let go of. A winter tree shows no obvious growth, a time of internal gestation in the unconscious. An evergreen tree shows a desire for change that is solid, stable and naturally occurring in all stages of growth.

Your **shelter** shows the personal identity you have created or are currently invested in. It might also be considered your protection, the meaning in your life, your life roles (i.e., teacher, parent, student, friend, etc.) or your ego. You might interpret the shelter in your drawing as showing a strong ego investment in your (mental/ spiritual/ emotional/ physical) life. *{Pick the appropriate word(s) depending upon which quadrant(s) your shelter is in.}* The door on your shelter tells about how you set limits. No door may indicate that you need to set more limits. Your window(s) shows willingness to look outside yourself and to have others look in. Your roof shows how you protect yourself, also how you put a ceiling on yourself. Is there a chimney for elimination? Is there a porch, for extending into nature?

The **bird** in your drawing shows your willingness to hear messages from within. Your bird shows where you have listened within and brought inner (mental/ spiritual/ emotional/ physical) messages to awareness and have taken action upon those images or guidance.

The **path** shows your ability to hope, to have a direction and a discipline. Your known directions and intentions at this time are (mental/ spiritual/ emotional/ physical). *{Pick the appropriate word(s) depending upon which quadrant(s) your path is in.}* What ground are you standing on? Our path is our discipline; even if we seem to be wandering, we still follow or create a path in the process. One path suggests you want to discover your own ways and structures without entrapment or advice. A divided path may show you are at a crossroads, facing a decision regarding two issues, directions or people. A symbol in the fork or the fork's location in the (mental/ spiritual/ emotional/ physical) quadrant of your drawing may show more about what the decision is about.

The **mountain** is a symbol of spirituality. It shows how a person is seeking or questing or dreaming for something greater than self, or for essential authenticity. The mountain in your drawing shows a quest, perhaps unknown to you consciously, in a (mental/ spiritual/ emotional/ physical) area of your life.

The **butterfly** is a symbol of major (mental/ spiritual/ emotional/ physical) changes that you have experienced or are currently completing. Memory of these major changes can help you in making other changes.

YOUR PROCESS OF DRAWING

Did you forget a symbol? Is this part of yourself you are outgrowing or overlooking? We tend to discard aspects of ourselves that we have outgrown, but what we need to do is to incorporate them.

What symbol did you have the most difficulty executing? If you had to spend more time with one symbol, it may depict a part of your life that requires extra attention now.

What sequence did you use? Your first symbol indicates a process that you know is going on - one that you are conscious of and that is important to you.

INTERACTION OF SYMBOLS

Two symbols interacting in your drawing have a definite relationship. Four examples follow.

1. The butterfly on another symbol shows the memory of successful completed change (butterfly) is helping you change your identity (butterfly on shelter) or helping you unfold (butterfly on flower).

2. The shelter on top of the mountain suggests your dream/quest (mountain) will lead to identity (shelter). The shelter lower down the mountain suggests your identity (shelter) will lead to your quest (mountain).

3. Your path on a mountain indicates that your quest (mountain) will be pursued with order, focus and discipline (path). If your path just goes to the base of the mountain, you don't yet know what you'll do with the quest.

4. Your snake and tree interacting show a major area of growth and change because the tree symbolizes the whole life growth process and the snake depicts death/rebirth.

MAKING YOUR OWN INTERPRETATION

Ultimately, the most important key for using your drawing as a diagnostic tool is to trust and use your own intuition. Use the above guidelines as starting points for awareness. From there, trust yourself.

Appendix C
I-WANT-LISTS

I-WANTS CHANGE OUR EXPERIENCES

Conscious goals (such as I-Wants) strongly affect not only life experiences but also our unconscious selves. For your unconscious (by means of dreams, creativity, ESP, higher-self work, etc.) will lead you into situations and relationships that help you toward or show you the folly/ inappropriateness of your conscious goals. This unconscious work is not usually obvious to our conscious minds.

It has become fashionable with some to believe that goals are not spontaneous and therefore wrong. The result of believing this can be years of wandering through life in a stuck no-goal rut without a full measure of life satisfaction. It is a dilemma at times whether to continue to follow our goals or set new ones. It is also true that goals can become stuck ruts that we doggedly follow to our detriment, but this is the result of clinging to outmoded goals. Goals are often in need of revision as we change or as our life circumstances change. Therefore, a regular review of all goals is recommended.

An example might help. If we set out driving from New York to Los Angeles, we may change our homesick minds in New Jersey or be called back by business or family matters. It is when we invest our goals with our expectations that we have strong reactions to their collapse. Important goals need not be the source of unhappiness or stress, even in the face of major roadblocks to their fruition (see Chapter 8). We will not be unhappy or upset about our aborted trip from New York to Los Angeles unless we have prior significant expectations for the trip or for Los Angeles. Even in that case, an attitude of "it is no doubt for the best" will prevent significant upset.

QUESTIONS & ANSWERS @ I-WANT-LISTS

How many I-Wants on a list?

The fewer the number, the more likely they will come true. We can only tackle a few life challenges at a time. Therefore, more than three or four I-Wants on your list will probably dilute your efforts.

But what if I want more than four?

I suggest that you (1)make a "Possible I-Wants" list, (2)remind yourself in your appointment book to consult this list monthly, and then (3)do so. You may choose then to place one or more of these possibilities on your current I-Want-List by removing a current listing. Do not tell yourself you *will* attempt these possible I-Wants, just that they are future possibilities. (Having *intentions* to do them will rob you of energy for doing today's list of I-Wants.)

What type of I-Wants work best?

The phrasing is important. We often create I-Wants that will prove to be similar to the above-described trip from NY-LA, aborted. Therefore, whenever possible, phrase your I-Want to be in the form of, "I want to be comfortable with my relationship," instead of "I want to get married." Or "I want to be comfortable with whatever anger I have," instead of "I want no anger."

What about my fears?

Fears surface in most processes of change. You will need to face them and somehow move beyond them, either (1)by seeing their lack of validity, (2)by doing what you fear anyhow, or (3)by self-growth or paid-for therapy.

MAKING YOUR I-WANT COME TRUE

(1) Make your I-Want come true by pretending.

Pretend (or visualize) the goal of comfort or peacefulness (instead of anger). It is the pretending that is vital and highly instrumental in making your I-Want come true. Pretend your goals are already realized - it may take some time for reality to match your pretending. If you have a goal of manifesting more money, it is often useful to **act** as if you had more - spend the extra dollar on yourself or give it to the next homeless person you meet.

(2) Write it down, say it aloud, and post it!

To manifest your I-Want, make sure you write it down, preferably in bold letters suitable for posting in a conspicuous place (or a private place where you would see it frequently). Say it aloud several times a day as you pass by this conspicuous place.

(3) Reward yourself.

Give yourself rewards often for beginning and intermediate steps. Rewards often fail because they are inappropriately selected or applied. For important information on rewards, see Appendix E.

YOUR GROWTH PROCESS

The use of this I-Want-List method will produce significant change in you, but it may require that you pursue very different paths than you originally anticipate. Also, there may be detours along the road as well as stuck places that seem impossible. Growth, like a country road, is sometimes muddy. But keep on slogging, for the sun shines most on those who persevere intelligently.

Appendix D
DO-IT-YOURSELF ALLERGY TESTING

CAUTION- before any major change in diet, consult with your physician.

TESTING YOURSELF

Doing the testing yourself for addictive food allergy is not that difficult; our bodies show stronger reactions to such substances after their consumption has been stopped for five or more days. Four possible testing methods:

(1) Dr. Mandell offers a five-day fast (Mandell and Scanlon 1979, 251) as one test alternative to make sure that no offending substances are consumed. After five days one food at a time is reintroduced (one meal = only one food) and the bodily reactions noted (including handwriting).

(2) A second alternative suggested, (Mandell and Scanlon 1979, 38), is a Rotary Diversified Diet. For five days one food is eaten at each meal (one meal = only one food), and this food is then repeated as the only food eaten at a particular meal five days later. Bodily reactions are noted.

(3) For those who are a bit lazier (like me), another alternative (which may contain accuracy pitfalls) is to consume only 1-2 foods for five days. Perhaps you might select lamb and rice or just rice without spices, oils, or dressings of any kind. (For most people rice is an unlikely allergy, and addictive allergy to lamb is unlikely because we rarely consume it.) Complex foods such as bread, casseroles, sauces etc. CANNOT be used as one of these 1-2 foods, because they contain several foods to which we may be allergic. Likewise, none on the list of most commonly encountered food offenders listed in Chapter 6 should be one of these 1-2 foods. After five days those 1-2 foods are stopped, and reactions are noted as one new food at a time is reintroduced.

(4) To test for one particular food, eliminate it entirely from your diet for five days and then reintroduce it to your diet. This may require close examination of all food labels in order to eliminate that one food for five days. Total elimination is essential; even the smallest amount of cheating, intended or unintended, will invalidate the test.

My personal recommendation, after trying the fasting method, would be to avoid the fast. (If you choose fasting, please read Dr. Mandell's four fasting cautions and warnings; and a consultation with your own physician beforehand is recommended.) Aside from physical weakness, my withdrawal symptoms of 'yuckiness' and 'irritability' were distinctly unpleasant during my fast. My hunger pangs were not difficult because I knew not to 'cheat' by stealing even a nibble; for cheating makes such hunger pangs rage to the extent that one might well have to give up a fast entirely. Without cheating, such hunger pains dissipate after a day or so. There are both pleasant and unpleasant reactions encountered in this allergy testing. The removal of those foods to which you are addictively allergic may cause both physical and psychological withdrawal symptoms, but ridding your system of substances to which you are allergic will tend to promote a strong sense of well-being. So do not expect that you will feel as usual in the process of testing no matter what method of testing you choose. For you may feel much better, you may feel somewhat worse, or you may feel both better and worse simultaneously.

PERSONAL EXAMPLE

For me, one particular side effect of my testing was very welcome, **the permanent loss of 8 pounds of body weight and 1 1/2 inches around each thigh**. These desirable effects were caused by eliminating peanuts and substances derived from peanuts from my diet. My allergy to peanuts (including peanut oil) had been unknown to me before testing. In fact, until I did the test myself, I counted myself among those who believed that allergies were likely just to be "in the head" of the sufferer. Needless to say, my compassion for those suffering with allergies has increased.

My peanut-eating patterns before allergy testing were typical of someone with addictive food allergies. I loved peanut butter, ate peanuts often, and my favorite candy bars usually contained peanuts in some form. I never went more than two days without consuming some form of peanuts. Cravings would compel me to make the next peanut butter sandwich. What happens with addictive food allergies is that after a day or so without the substance we tend to suffer withdrawal symptoms and tend to crave the substance. Just a small amount of the substance will usually give us our 'fix' and we can then go on for a day or two without more of it. What happens is that this 'fix' prevents our withdrawal symptoms. In my case, the withdrawal symptoms were "yuckiness" and "irritability". The heightened allergic reaction brought about by five days of abstinence from peanuts, which I never had experienced until the testing reintroduced peanuts, was a deep joint pain lasting for many hours after consumption of peanuts. I had never considered myself to be allergic to anything, but this pain thoroughly convinced me that it was too difficult for my body to continue to consume peanuts. This was the only strong allergy I found for myself, though I did react mildly to both dairy and yeast.

While reintroducing foods during my testing, a lack of time as well as laziness led me to introduce new foods every three hours rather than just three times a day. If you decide to change your testing in a similar fashion, beware the long-term reaction(s) which may be masked by the introduction of a new food three hours later. Retesting five days later may be required for those particular foods whose test results may have become confused.

Reminder- food allergy can without our knowledge cause most any "psychological" symptom.

Appendix E
GOALS & REWARDS

CHANGING BEHAVIOR PERMANENTLY

We all know how easy it sometimes is to make a temporary behavior change such as starting a new diet or exercise program. Then after a few days or hours, our drive fizzles, our will weakens, we "cheat" a bit, and our new program is discarded like last year's New Year's resolutions.

Using goals and rewards effectively will improve your chances for making such changes permanent.

INTERMEDIATE SMALL GOALS

We tend to make a grand pronouncement of a large goal such as: "I am going to lose 60 pounds." While it is productive to have an overall goal, we usually need smaller intermediate goals along the way. These might be a goal of (1)adding carrots or other vegetables three times a day in a weight loss program, (2)one stretching exercise every day in an exercise program, or (3)sobriety one day at a time as emphasized by AA.

Perhaps you might set a goal of pretending three times a day that your desired goal is occurring right now. This pretending will effectively lead you to whatever stumbling blocks are in your path. (Your attitudes are crucial - if you believe you will fail, you most likely will. Also, emphasizing the unhappiness of your current situation tends to dig a deeper rut for yourself.)

Thus, success will more likely be yours if you (1)**set beginning and intermediate small goals** and (2) **practice pretending these goals are already true.**

REWARDS ARE IMPORTANT

One of the best ways to aid the change process is through a system of rewards. Rewards give a sense of satisfaction and accomplishment in the midst of trials that are customarily encountered when significant behavior change is attempted. Assume that you are trying to change some behavior concerning food or exercise. "Just a nibble" or "Maybe I'll just skip exercising today" are thoughts that will surely come to mind. If you feel good because you have rewarded yourself for having accomplished your goal yesterday, you are much more likely to resist the temptations of the old behavior today.

What type of rewards work best? Do you remember the colored/ gold stars your elementary teacher used on your school papers? Something as simple as a gold star will be effective. The reward must be visible and able to be seen by you as you pass by it several times a day. It is the visibility and meaning that is important, not the reward itself. An added penny/ shell/ bean on a kitchen shelf every time you accomplish your desired behavior will do fine. (Or post a page on your refrigerator and use stars/ colored dots/ large check marks.)

In the beginning, make the reward frequent so that the pennies on your shelf keep adding up. If that is not feasible, keep your rewards visible for a full week. Reward yourself for parts of the desired change. For example, give yourself one reward for stretching before exercising and one reward for exercising instead of one reward for both. Intermediate goals might be such things as a hot bath, a massage, a movie, coffee with an old friend, etc.

Rewards that will usually <u>not</u> work are those that involve food, or those that reverse the pennies on the shelf idea (i.e., set up 7 pennies on the shelf at the beginning of the week and *take away* a penny each time you exercise during the week).

In short, make your rewards: (1)**visible** and (2)**often**.

RELAPSES

Relapses are often encountered. Usually your best actions when faced with a relapse into old unwanted behavior are: (1)to smile, (2)to tell yourself that relapses happen to most people and (3)to restart your change program (perhaps with small modifications). Too often, we respond to a relapse as if it meant permanent failure.

When changing our behaviors,
we often need to be
patient with ourselves.

Appendix F
OUIJA BOARD FOR PSYCHIC KLUTZES

DON'T LET SKEPTICISM BE YOUR TYRANT

Consider for a moment that you can easily try out the ouija board in the privacy of your home for a total cost of 0-25 cents. You do not have to purchase special equipment or spend more than a few minutes.

But you do need to suspend old prejudices for about half an hour to discover what you might learn today from this rather ancient spiritual tool. You will probably be unsuccessful at the ouija board, if you let skepticism be your tyrant. (If it doesn't work for you after experimentation, then you can resume your old prejudices about it.)

One theory that explains ouija board phenomena is that there are guides for us who can be accessed via this board. (Consider your guide to be a higher being, your higher self or some other more-knowing entity.) The board is a mechanical tool that allows such a guide to communicate more readily. A recent poll indicated that about 50% of us now believe in ESP, so there is a good chance that you, the reader, no longer strongly resist the idea of such communication. Why not allow yourself to play at the ouija board? I long considered myself a psychic klutz, yet a homemade ouija board (with thanks to my friend Pauline for the idea) as described below did eventually work for me.

FIVE MINUTE CONSTRUCTION PROJECT

Construction of your own ouija board can take as little as five minutes with paper and scissors. Why not make your own right now? (Please remember that ouija-board prettiness is irrelevant to your guide.)

1. **Copy the next two facing pages of this book.** (By xerox or by hand is OK- your copy does not need to have the letters be perfectly formed). *It is important that each letter of the alphabet be visible. The reason for copies is that flatness is desirable, not the curved surfaces of these book pages.*

2. **Place your xerox copy under a piece of clear plastic** (file folder, photo album, plexiglass, clear glass, etc. will do fine) so that a plastic lid from a small container (yogurt, margarine, etc.) will glide easily across the surface of the clear plastic. *This easy movement of the plastic lid is important.*

3. **Turn your plastic lid into a pointer.** If you can't see through your lid, cut a hole in it with scissors or knife. (jagged or perfectly round hole OK) *a hole slightly larger than the size of the letters of the alphabet on your homemade ouija board.* If your plastic lid is clear, make an X in the center of your lid with a magic marker or crayon. This modified plastic lid is now your *pointer,* used to point out individual letters on the oiuja board. Your homemade ouija board is now ready. Are you?

Caution: all messages may not be the truth- verify, verify, verify!

GENERAL INSTRUCTIONS

People work the ouija board in various ways. For some, their pointer (plastic lid) flies all over the board, and they can do it with their eyes closed. For others, like this author, using the pointer to deliberately scan the letters with eyes open (or shut) will yield *some mild bodily reaction* (in a hand, arm, shoulder or elsewhere) when the correct letter is scanned. Experiment to find your best method.

Try resting the fingertips of your *non-writing* hand on your pointer and practice gliding the pointer over the letters for a few seconds trying various scanning methods. This allows you to write with one hand the letters which your guide is communicating to you, while your other hand remains on the pointer. It is important that *your pointing arm and hand be in a comfortable position,* for your bodily reactions (telling you the correct letter being communicated) will often be masked by bodily discomfort. This might mean sitting in such a way that the ouija board is on hard surface like a table.

There are potential difficulties encountered in operating the board. (1)Stress, lack of relaxation, depression, or being "out of sorts" in any way will probably prevent successful communication. (2)When the board *does* start giving messages, then sometimes, particularly in the beginning, we get excited or misread a particular letter. This can throw us off entirely. (3)Your guide is the being with whom you wish to communicate. Not being specific about with whom you wish to communicate can result in failure or contact with "unhelpful" beings. If this occurs, ask for *your* guide. (4)The ouija board is usually not right for us continuously. Periods of fallowness are common, for days or months at a time. (5)If the future is just a probablility based upon our upcoming choices, then there really are no 100% clearcut "answers" about the future. Thus, it's better to ask "How can I be more prosperous?" than "Will I be rich?"

ARE YOU READY TO WORK THE OUIJA BOARD NOW?

1. **Preparation of oneself.** Place your homemade board and pointer on a hard surface nearby or in front of you. *Try relaxing or meditating for a few minutes so that your mind can be as cleared as possible of routine matters and distractions.*

2. **Ask for guidance from your guide.** Silent asking is OK, for it is your intent which is important. ("I want to communicate with my guide" is fine.)

3. **Ask specific questions.** Questions that can be answered with a yes/no reply are often easier because the reply need not be spelled out. Ask a specific question such as "Do you have any suggestions for me about my problem X?" Then, scan the board with your pointer. If your hand doesn't seem to want to stop at a particular letter or yes/no response, then try deliberately moving your pointer slowly over the letters from A to Z and also over the yes/no responses to see if you can sense a bodily reaction when the pointer points to a particular letter or to yes/no. If the board answers "yes", then the next question can be "*what* suggestions do you have for me about my problem X?" (Failure? Try again over the next two weeks perhaps once every 2-3 days for five minutes at a time. Still failure? It is probably not right for you now. Give it up until the impulse strikes to try it again.) Keep experimenting! Practice does make for more proficiency.

247

ABCDEFG

NOPQRST

YES   1 2 3
7 8

248

HIJKLM

UVWXYZ

4 5 6   NO
9 0

Bibliography

Bailey, Covert. *Fit or Fat*. Boston: Houghton Mifflin, 1978.

Barbach, Lonnie G. *For Yourself: The Fulfillment of Female Sexuality*. New York: Doubleday, 1975.

Bennett, William J. *The Devaluing of America*. New York: Simon and Schuster, 1992.

Bradshaw, John. *Homecoming*. New York: Bantam, 1992.

Chopra, Deepak, M.D. *Ageless Body, Timeless Mind*. New York: Harmony, 1993.

Dyer, Wayne W. *You'll See It When You Believe It*. New York: W. Morrow, 1989.

Egoscue, Pete. *The Egoscue Method of Health Through Motion*. New York: Harper-Collins, 1992.

Fezler, William D. *Creative Imagery; How to Visualize in All Five Senses*. New York: Simon and Schuster, 1989.

Hay, Louise L. *You Can Heal Your Life*. Santa Monica: Hay House, 1984.

Kaufman, Barry N. *To Love Is to be Happy With*. New York: Ballantine, 1978. _____*Happiness Is a Choice*. New York: Ballantine, 1991. (Barry Kaufman's books available through the Option Institute, 2080 S. Undermountain Rd. Sheffield, MA 01257.)

Kopp, Sheldon B. *If You Meet the Buddha on the Road, Kill Him*. Palo Alto, CA: Science and Behavior, 1972.

Mandell, Marshall, M.D., and Scanlon, Lynne W. *5-Day Allergy Relief System*. New York: Crowell, 1979.

Monroe, Robert A. *Journeys Out of the Body*. New York: Doubleday, 1971.

Morehouse, Laurence E., and Gross, Leonard. *Total Fitness in 30 Minutes a Week*. New York: Simon and Schuster, 1975.

O'Neill, George and Nena. *Open Marriage; A New Life Style for Couples*. New York: M. Evans, 1972.

Oxford American Dictionary. New York: Avon, 1980.

Peck, M. Scott, M.D. *The Road Less Traveled*. New York: Simon and Schuster, 1978.

Roberts, Jane. *Seth Speaks; The Eternal Validity of the Soul*. Englewood Cliffs, NJ: Prentice-Hall, 1972.
_____ *The Nature of Personal Reality*. Englewood Cliffs, NJ: Prentice-Hall, 1974.

Sakoian, Frances, and Acker, Louis S. *The Astrologer's Handbook*. New York: Harper and Row, 1973.

Segal, Erich. *Love Story*. New York: Harper and Row, 1970.

Siegel, Bernie S. *Love, Medicine & Miracles*. New York: Harper & Row, 1986.

Sinetar, Marsha. *Do What You Love, The Money Will Follow*. New York: Paulist Press, 1987.

Steinem, Gloria. *Revolution from Within: A Book of Self-Esteem*. Boston: Little, Brown and Co., 1992.

Wambach, Helen. *Reliving Past Lives: The Evidence Under Hypnosis*. New York: Harper and Row, 1978.

Weiss, Brian L., M.D. *Through Time into Healing*. New York: Simon and Schuster, 1992

Yarbro, Chelsea Q. *Messages from Michael*. New York: Berkley, 1979.

Zilbergeld, Bernie. *The New Male Sexuality*. New York: Bantam, 1992.

Index

A

B

C

---

*See first paragraph on page 5.

*See first paragraph on page 5.

---

*See first paragraph on page 5.

*See first paragraph on page 5.

*See first paragraph on page 5.

*See first paragraph on page 5.

About the Author

Therapist and author, Thayer White, has over 23 years experience as both therapist and client in the areas of therapy and self-growth.

Thayer is licensed to do psychotherapy in California as a Marriage Family and Child Counselor. He received his master's degree in Transpersonal Counseling Psychology from John F. Kennedy University (in Orinda, California), and his bachelor's degree from Northwestern University (in Evanston, Illinois).

Since licensure, the majority of his therapy clients have been other therapists and their family members who have come to him to *resolve* longstanding issues. He is a past president of his local 200+ member therapist organization, the San Francisco Chapter of the California Association of Marriage and Family Therapists.

He brings two important personal characteristics, creativity and a sense of humor, to this self-help psychology book. These attributes often seem to be missing from other books in the field. In the Michael teaching, he is an old scholar with a goal of acceptance. On the Enneagram he is a point five, the observer. Astrologically he is an Aries, with Libra rising and a Scorpio moon.

Notes

Notes

Ordering Information

If you wish to order a copy of this book, you may do so

    1. by phoning **1-800-481-4891** or

    2. by FAXing **1-415-468-6004** or

    3. by writing Purple Paradox Press, Box 347172, San Francisco, CA., 94134.

When ordering, please provide the following information:

Name _____

Street/PO Address _____

City/State/ZIP _____

Phone (_ _ _)_ _ _ _-_ _ _ _

If paying by MC____ or VISA____ (indicate which)

        MC/VISA #_____

        MC/VISA expiration date _____

Cost is $16 (US funds by check, money order, or VISA/MC) which includes all state sales taxes, shipping and handling. If outside USA, additional charges may apply.